STUDY SKILLS

for *Learning*
Power

Regina Hellyer

Carol Robinson

Phyllis Sherwood

English Department
Raymond Walters College
of the University of Cincinnati

HOUGHTON MIFFLIN COMPANY   **Boston**   **New York**

Assistant Editor: Melissa Plumb
Associate Project Editor: Christina Lillios
Senior Production/Design Coordinator: Carol Merrigan
Manufacturing Coordinator: Marie Barnes
Editorial Assistant: Joy Park

COVER IMAGE: Clockwise from top: © Yugi Matsumoto/35mm/Photonica; © Naoki Kimura/Photonica; © Beverly Brown/Photonica; © Minori Kawana/Photonica.
COVER DESIGN: Rebecca Fagan

TEXT CREDITS: Page 42, From Levine and Miller, *Biology: Discovering Life*, Second Edition. Copyright © 1994 by D.C. Heath and Company. Used by permission of Houghton Mifflin Company;   page 55, from *Concentration: Strategies for Attaining Focus* by Becky Patterson. Copyright © 1993 by Kendall/Hunt Publishing Company. Used with permission;   page 61, Untitled poem #1263 by Emily Dickinson from *The Complete Poems of Emily Dickinson*, ed. Thomas H. Johnson. Reprinted by permission of Little, Brown and Company;   page 68, from Sylvia S. Mader, *Inquiry into Life*, 7th edition. Copyright © 1994 Times Mirror Higher Education Group. Inc., Dubuque, IA. All rights reserved. Reprinted by permission;   page 76, copyright © 1981 by Houghton Mifflin Company. Reproduced by permission from *The American Heritage Dictionary of the English Language*;   page 84, entry for "attend" from *Roget's International Thesaurus*, 4th edition, revised by Robert L. Chapman. Copyright © 1977 by Harper & Row, Publisher, Inc., Reprinted by permission of HarperCollins Publishers, Inc.;   page 84, copyright © 1995 by Houghton Mifflin Company. Reproduced by permission from *Roget's II: The New Thesaurus, Third Edition*;   page 104, *The Little Engine That Could* and *I think I can, I think I can* are trademarks of Platt & Munk, Publishers and are used by permission;   pp. 130–131, from *Take Control of Your Life* by Sharon Faelten and David Diamond. Copyright © 1988 by Rodale Press. Reprinted by permission   pp. 140–141, Excerpts: "First Things First" from *Efficient Study Strategies: Skills for Successful Learning* by George M. Usova. Pacific Grove, CA: Brooks/Cole Publishing Company, 1989;   pp. 181–182, from *Introduction to Child Development*, 4th edition, by John P. Dworetzky. Copyright © 1990 by West Publishing. Reprinted by permission.

Copyright © 1998 by Houghton Mifflin Company. All rights reserved.

Printed in the U.S.A.

Student Text ISBN: 0-395-73856-3

123456789-QF-01 00 99 98 97

As part of Houghton Mifflin's ongoing commitment to the environment, this text has been printed on recycled paper.

Table of Contents

Preface

We wrote *Study Skills for Learning Power* to fulfill the needs of our students. Although many study skills books were available, none of them was quite right for our course and our students. We needed a concise, practical, readable, down-to-earth, student-oriented, hands-on, reader-friendly book. We wanted the students to use the study skills as they learned them, rather than complacently to read theories about study techniques. The ultimate goal was to have students put critical thinking into action as they learned. We made a concerted effort to set an appropriate tone, using vocabulary suitable for all college students. We are confident that we have met our objectives because students using this book have stated that the book seems to "talk to them," is very easy to understand, and has given them practical strategies to make positive changes in their academic lives.

Study Skills for Learning Power is an interactive textbook. To us, interactive learning means participatory learning. Two major areas that make this book participatory are the format and the exercises. We have designed the format of the pages with extra-wide margins so students can practice using STUDY-READ (Chapter 3). We also created exercises that encourage students to search their experiences and knowledge as a basis for acquiring new skills and strategies. In the final analysis, the true test of interactiveness involves having students apply their new skills in all their other courses.

Not only is *Study Skills for Learning Power* student-friendly; it is also teacher-friendly. All chapters are autonomous, so that they can be taught according to teachers' preferences, or studied according to students' needs. We realize that each chapter is necessary to a student's success and could be considered the one chapter students should read and understand first. Because each chapter can stand alone, teachers can make their own decisions about the chapter order they will use.

Study Skills for Learning Power lends itself well to a variety of courses, namely, the freshman-year experience, freshman orientation, study skills, effective reading and study skills, the college seminar, pre-college workshops, and summer study programs. The textbook can be adapted readily to a quarter or semester system or a year-long seminar with students typically earning one, two, or three credit hours.

Instructors might note that an *Instructor's Resource Manual* is available. It contains sample syllabi for courses of various lengths and chapter-by-chapter information, including suggestions for teaching and classroom activities, answers to exercises, as well as factual quiz questions and critical thinking application questions. In addition, we have included transparency masters for each chapter and an extensive test bank, organized by chapter content and by types of questions (definition, true-false, multiple choice, essay, etc.) from which instructors can design their own tests. Finally, we provide a bibliography for each chapter for those interested in doing further reading and research.

The title of our book, *Study Skills for Learning Power,* comes from the belief that students have the power within themselves to take control of their own learning. This textbook, along with an instructor's guide, serves as a catalyst to this end.

Acknowledgments

Our thanks go first to the many students we have taught over the years. We certainly have learned as much from them as we have taught them. Their questions, comments, concerns, and needs guided us to formulate the contents of this textbook. A special thanks to those students who allowed us to quote them throughout the book.

Next, we wish to thank the reading and study skills monitors, tutors, and lab staff at Raymond Walters College for their emotional support, information, and analytical skills. Specifically, we thank: Denise Albert, Janet Baril, Pam Bauer, Beverly Claunch, Della Colmar, Mary McClellan, Vivian McCracken, Maureen Nestor, Diane Skie, Paula Spievack, and Judy Whitton. We realize it took courage on their part to walk the fine line between critiquing our writing and hurting our feelings.

We are especially grateful to Mary McClellan for her precise critiquing of our text, to Ann Chisko for her assistance in writing the section on reading math, and to Beverly Claunch and Janet Baril for assistance in the section on reading in the sciences.

We offer a round of applause and special gratitude to John Sherwood who allowed us to transform first his living room and then most of the rest of his house into our office and who gave us food for thought—gourmet style.

We would also like to thank the following reviewers who helped us in creating this book: Bill Baker, Broward Community College (FL); Leslie Kaufman, Burlington County College (NJ); Victor Paul Keleman Jr., North Lake College (TX); E. James Petty, Clarke College (IA); Barbara Swanson, Idaho State University; Annette Woods, Sinclair Community College (OH).

Introduction

Study Skills for Learning Power is designed to provide you with skills and strategies to enable you to gain learning power, power for success in college as well as in life. Each chapter deals with necessary skills, learning concepts, and helpful tips and shows you how to use them to your advantage. In this introduction, we will briefly describe the contents of each chapter and explore some myths about college.

SUMMARY OF TEXT

Chapter 1, "The Power of Note Taking," describes one of the most important skills for a successful college student. As soon as you begin any course, you will need to keep a clear record of lectures, dialogues, and interactions in every class. The GREAT Note Taking System provides you with five steps that supply you with an excellent method of note taking and studying that will ensure your mastery of the material.

Chapter 2, "The Power of Reading for Meaning," defines various types of reading and explains why reading rates should be adjusted for different purposes. This chapter also discusses main ideas, major and minor support, and patterns of organization. It also helps you discover how to read and understand visual aids.

Chapter 3, "The Power of STUDY-READING," begins with a system you can use to evaluate your textbooks. This chapter provides you with a method for reading chapter assignments called STUDY-READ, a systematic way to read and study the textbook information.

Chapter 4, "The Power of Words," reviews the important ways the dictionary can be useful to you and offers three techniques for learning vocabulary and technical terms in your courses.

Chapter 5, "The Power of Self-Knowledge," allows you to determine what kind of learner you are—auditory, visual, or tactile, what your personality type is, and how to use this knowledge to your best advantage. In addition, you will discover ways to be more self-motivated.

Chapter 6, "The Power of Managing Goals, Problems, and Stress," discusses how to set short- and long-term goals, explains how to SOLVE problems, defines stress, and offers suggestions for dealing with stress.

Chapter 7, "The Power of Time Management," encourages you to become time "wise" and more efficient and organized in how you spend your time. This chapter gives examples of several different scheduling systems.

Chapter 8, "The Power of Memory," provides you with ways to improve your long-term memory and to increase your powers of concentration. It also demonstrates how to remember difficult concepts or material by using various memory techniques.

Chapter 9, "The Power of Making Your Own Visual Organizers," offers several methods for organizing large amounts of information visually, which will allow you to study efficiently for exams.

Chapter 10, "The Power of Taking Tests," reviews methods that should enable you to become better at taking objective, short answer, and essay tests. The chapter includes ways to minimize test anxiety and a method to analyze test results.

By the time you finish this course, understanding the material in this text will empower you to be a successful college student—the rest is up to you. But first, let's clear up some common myths about college.

MYTHS ABOUT COLLEGE

1. **Since many professors in college do not take attendance, I can skip classes when I want to or need to. It's not a big deal if I am there or not.**

   Get real! Would you say that about seeing your favorite rock star live and in concert versus hearing a CD? Would you say that about experiencing the Fourth of July fireworks display vs. watching it on TV? The old saying holds true: "You have to be there."

2. **If I am a full-time college student, I only need to attend classes approximately twelve to fifteen hours a week; therefore, I can easily hold a full-time job outside of school and fulfill my family obligations.**

   You've got to be kidding! Even Superman and Wonder Woman have to eat and sleep sometime.

3. **Reading is reading. The way I read a textbook is really no different from the way I read a magazine, a newspaper, or a novel.**

   Dream on! It's a matter of purpose, approach, and accountability. Would you want your doctor to read medical journals the same way he/she would read *Sports Illustrated*?

4. **If a professor does not collect my homework or check up on my reading assignments through quizzes, then I don't need to worry about doing any of those assignments.**

   Hakuna Matata! If you don't worry about homework, maybe you won't need to worry about graduation, either.

5. **If I don't like a particular required class or if I get too far behind in a class, it is best to just stop attending. The teacher really won't care if I disappear, and I can take the course some other time.**

   Think again! A computer never forgets. When your body disappears, your name doesn't disappear from the registration records.

6. **In college, my success in a given course depends mostly upon the professor's teaching abilities. If he or she cannot hold my interest, it's not my problem.**

   Oops! If this were true, your high-school driving instructor would be responsible when you run over your first pedestrian.

7. **If I attend classes and do all my homework in a course, then I am guaranteed a passing grade.**

   Sorry, Charlie! Life has no guarantees. The only sure things in life are death and taxes. Seriously, no doubt attending classes and doing homework are extremely important. However, you still have to demonstrate mastery of the course by passing tests.

8. **Learning in college is a snap. All I have to do is memorize.**

   Whoa! Would you call yourself Picasso just because you've memorized the primary colors? Could you take Jerry Garcia's place with the Grateful Dead just because you've memorized the notes of the musical scale?

9. **If I ask for a conference with a teacher outside of class, he/she might think that I'm not smart enough to be in the course.**

   Go for it! Silence may be golden, but not when dealing with doctors or teachers.

10. **Tutoring and learning centers in college are not for regular students like me.**

    Don't kid yourself! Presidents and kings use cabinet members and advisors. Shouldn't you take advantage of experts, too?

11. **If I arrive late for class or leave early, it's no big deal.**

    Come on! Try telling that to Delta Airlines.

12. **All lists should be written in even numbers.**

    Oh, yeah? That's another myth!

Chapter 1

The Power of Note Taking

One of the most important skills you need in college is the ability to take good notes. In this chapter, you will learn why you should take notes and the importance of listening. Not only will you learn how to take good notes, but you will learn how to take GREAT notes.

THE EBBINGHAUS FORGETTING CURVE

Have you ever started to tell a joke and then realized that you could not remember the punch line? Has an appointment ever slipped your mind? Have you ever sat in a classroom and listened to an interesting lecture, only to forget the details the next day? Have you ever taken a test and forgotten an important bit of information? Most of you will answer yes to all these questions because you do forget on occasion; that is only human.

In the late 1800s, Hermann Ebbinghaus, a psychologist, studied forgetfulness by researching the human mind and its ability to remember new information. Because of his thoroughness and precision in studying the human memory, his findings are still considered valid today and are often cited in basic psychology and study skills textbooks, as well as in books about memory. Although some numbers vary slightly in different texts, the results, called the Ebbinghaus Forgetting Curve (Loftus 67), look like this:

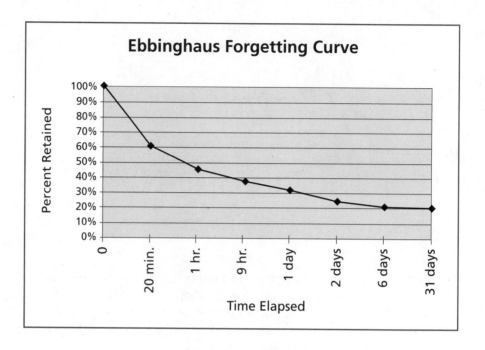

From the Ebbinghaus Forgetting Curve, you can see that within twenty minutes you are likely to forget approximately 40 percent of what you hear or read, and by the time twenty-four hours have elapsed, you may have forgotten almost 70 percent. It is rather frightening to think that you can forget more than half of what you have heard or read in one day.

Knowing this information, you will not be surprised by the following conversation between Will and Karen:

"Hey, Will, how did you do on the psych test?"

"Oh, man, I really bombed that one! I don't know what happened. I went to class and read the book, but I couldn't remember a thing!" Will moaned.

"Well, maybe your notes were lousy. After all, the test was mostly on the lectures," Karen said. "Let me see your notes."

"Notes? What notes?" Will said indignantly. "I don't take notes! I go to class and listen."

"I listen, too, but I can't remember unless I write it down," Karen responded.

Will is not unique in his ability to forget. The Ebbinghaus Forgetting Curve indicates that everyone has a tendency to forget a great deal. In fact, the Ebbinghaus Curve shows that a month after hearing a lecture or reading an assignment, you may have forgotten up to 80 percent of what you heard or read—not good news in terms of taking exams.

However, by using good study skills, you can reverse this forgetting trend and remember as much as 80 percent or more of what you hear or read. Cultivating this ability to remember requires listening carefully and taking effective notes during a lecture, skills that will be discussed in this chapter. In Chapters 2 and 3, you will learn how to improve your ability to remember what you read.

POWER LISTENERS AND PASSIVE LISTENERS

Power listeners are quite different from passive listeners. *Power listeners* are people who actively listen to what is being said. They realize that the classroom is a learning environment in which information is exchanged. Power listeners, like power walkers, are easily recognizable in class. They are intense, focused, and purposeful. They have the right equipment, the right attitude, and the right mental focus, not letting anything distract them from listening to a lecture. Just as power walkers appear to have everything working together to build a better body, power listeners have everything working together to build a better mind.

Passive listeners, on the other hand, physically hear the words being said, but they make little attempt to engage their minds to understand the message. Unlike power listeners, passive listeners are like window shoppers strolling through the mall. These listeners are occupying space in the classroom, relaxed and purposeless. They are filling in time and often seem to have this attitude: "OK, I'm here. Entertain me." To them, it is not themselves but the teacher who is responsible for their learning.

From the descriptions above, you can see that listening involves more than *just* hearing. Students' actions and attitudes are also important. Obviously, the power listener is going to get a great deal more out of class than the passive listener.

Take the following survey to determine what your actions and attitudes indicate about you in the classroom:

Exercise 1-A

Directions: Check the answers that best describe your behaviors and attitudes in your *least* interesting class.

	Always	Usually	Sometimes	Never
1. I arrive at class on time.	____	____	____	____
2. I have my homework completed.	____	____	____	____
3. I take lots of notes.	____	____	____	____
4. I look out the window.	____	____	____	____
5. I am distracted by other students.	____	____	____	____
6. My mind wanders in class.	____	____	____	____
7. I expect the teacher to be entertaining.	____	____	____	____
8. I work on homework for other classes in this class.	____	____	____	____
9. I think using a tape recorder is just as good as taking notes.	____	____	____	____
10. I sit in the front row.	____	____	____	____

If you answered questions 1, 2, 3, and 10 "always" or "usually" and questions 4, 5, 6, 7, 8, and 9 "sometimes" or "never," you are a power listener. If you did not, then you may need to reexamine your attitudes and behaviors so that you can get the most from your classes.

The examples that follow will provide you with models of power listeners and passive listeners.

Power Listeners

Jennifer and Dave are power listeners who begin preparing for class before they ever enter the classroom. They have done their homework, and they arrive on time, sometimes even a little early. If the class is the first of the day and they are commuters, they realize that they need to leave home early enough to allow for delays in driving, particularly in bad weather. By the time the instructor begins, they already have their notebooks open and their pens out, ready to take notes. They sit in the front of the room so that they will not be distracted by other students.

Both Jennifer's and Dave's behaviors in class increase their listening skills. Their body language, especially their posture, indicates positive attitudes. They make eye contact with the instructor when they are not taking notes. Because they are really listening to what the instructor has to say, their body language indicates that they are doing their best to comprehend the information. Jennifer sometimes nods when she clearly understands a point and frowns as she tries to grasp a difficult idea. Dave participates in class discussions and sometimes raises his hand to ask for further clarification during a lecture. They appreciate an interesting instructor, but they still pay attention even if the lecturer is dull. They are power listeners who take extensive notes.

Jennifer and Dave do not close their notebooks until after the instructor has finished speaking, even if it is a minute or so after class is supposed to end. They also know the simple rules of etiquette: The classroom is like a conversation—one person does not walk away (or pack up) while the other is speaking. They know the importance of getting as much out of the class as possible.

If, for some valid reason, Jennifer or Dave is unable to attend a class, each calls the other to ask for his or her notes, knowing that the notes will be comprehensive. As power listeners, they know the value of having a *study buddy,* someone they can rely on as a backup person, in every class.

Passive Listeners

Nancy and Frank are passive students. They don't always attend class, and when they do attend, they may not be prepared. They barely arrive on time or are even a few minutes late, so they don't have their notebooks out when the instructor begins speaking. To avoid being noticed by the instructor, they choose the most inconspicuous seats, such as those in the back row or on the fringe.

Both Nancy and Frank believe that since they have appeared in class, learning will magically happen. They slouch or lounge in their seats, gaze out the window, or check out their classmates. Nancy frequently looks at her watch, and Frank yawns and sometimes dozes off when the lecture is not "entertaining." They physically *hear* what is being said, but they do not mentally *listen*. Sometimes they do homework for another class. The few notes they take are buried under elaborate doodling.

About five minutes before class ends, Nancy and Frank begin getting ready to leave. They close their notebooks, unzip their backpacks, stuff everything in, and zip them up again. They are oblivious to the fact that the noise they are making is disturbing those around them. One or two minutes before class is over, Frank stands up and puts on his jacket. Nancy struggles into her coat while sitting in her chair. They are the first ones out the door.

One day Frank overslept and missed class. When he saw Nancy later in the day, he said, "Did I miss anything in class today?" "No," Nancy replied, "we just did the same old stuff." As passive listeners, neither Frank nor Nancy seems to realize the need for active participation and responsibility in the college classroom.

Exercise 1-B

Directions: List the characteristics of power listeners.

Column 1: Attitudes   **Column 2: Actions**

_____   _____

_____   _____

_____   _____

_____   _____

_____   _____

_____   _____

TAKING *GREAT* NOTES

Since you now know how easy it is to forget and what it takes to be a power listener, you need to learn how to take not just good notes but GREAT notes. Sure, you've been taking notes before this, but your system may not be as efficient and effective as it could be.

To begin an effective note-taking system, you must have the basic tools: summary paper and a three-ring binder with tabs to separate your notes for each class. Using a three-ring binder gives you great flexibility. One of the advantages of using a binder is that you can insert handouts, syllabi, homework, or other pages of information in the appropriate places for each class. Other advantages are that you can add to or change your notes easily and take out the pages you need to study instead of always carrying around the whole binder. Next, you need loose-leaf summary paper, that is, paper with a three-inch left margin. If you do not have summary paper, you can draw a line three inches from the left edge of your paper.

Note taking, the focus of this chapter, is a process that involves a great deal more than simply the physical act of writing. Not only does it help you remember information from your lectures, but it also helps you concentrate, condense information, and discover important points. It is a process that begins before class and lasts until you have mastered the information. Taking effective notes and reading textbooks are the two major means of receiving information in college.

All study skills books describe at least one system for taking notes. The GREAT note-taking system combines the best features of them all. GREAT is an acronym, a word formed from the first letter (in the case of wRite, the first audible letter) of each important word in a phrase. The letters G-R-E-A-T stand for the five steps in the note-taking process. Each letter in GREAT represents one step in the system. The five steps are:

Get ready

wRite

Edit

Ask questions

Test yourself

Step One: Get Ready

Preparing for note taking *before* you enter the classroom to hear a lecture is as important as the actual note taking itself. This preparation will directly affect the quality of your listening and note taking.

The Get-ready stage can be compared to preparing for a vacation trip. Before you go on a trip, you usually do some mental work, such as selecting your destination, deciding when to go, choosing a place to stay, deciding on transportation, reading about what sights are considered special enough to visit, and deciding what to pack. You usually make physical preparations as well if you want the trip to be successful, such as getting your car in good running order if you are driving, packing your suitcases, loading the car, or getting to the airport if you are flying.

Similar to making your vacation plan, you must prepare your *mind* before you enter the classroom. Getting ready to take notes involves three tasks that are performed before attending each class.

First, in order to Get ready, you must read your textbook assignment and do any other homework. (In Chapter 3 you will learn the most productive way to read your textbook assignments.)

Second, you need to review your notes from the previous lecture. When you have reviewed, you have the material in mind, which makes learning additional material easier because the human brain functions best when new information is attached to already learned ideas.

This ability to learn new information by relating it to something you already know can be demonstrated in several ways. Math courses, for example, are taught sequentially, with each new component building on the one before. In drawing classes you also start with simple figures and techniques and progress to more complex ones. In all learning situations, whether your previous knowledge is something you learned just minutes ago or years ago, your grasp of the new knowledge is enhanced by your previous knowledge, which creates a background of information. Thus, your mental preparation of reviewing your previous notes is an essential element of note taking. In fact, knowing that you are prepared will not only aid in your learning but also give you added confidence when class begins.

The third task in the Get-ready stage is a physical one: Make sure you have all the materials you will need for all of your classes. In addition to your binder and summary paper, you should bring to class your pens, textbooks, and other supplies, such as a calculator, a ruler, pencils, and any homework. Your backpack should serve as a portable desk, allowing you to get to work as soon as you enter the classroom.

Step Two: wRite

The second step, wRite, means to take notes during class. When the instructor arrives, have your notebook open and pen in hand. Put the date and page number in the top right-hand corner of your summary paper, and continue to do this on all subsequent pages. The illustration below shows the format of the summary paper you will be using to take notes in all your classes:

Three-inch column	Five-inch column	Date Page #
	You will be taking your	
	notes in this five-inch column	
	of summary	
	paper.	

To begin taking lecture notes, you need to focus all your attention on the speaker. Write down all pertinent information: main ideas, facts, details, examples, definitions, and even "common-sense" information—that is, information you think everyone should already know. Remember the Ebbinghaus Forgetting Curve: Even if you think you will remember something, chances are it will be gone before the day is over because you have only been exposed to the information; you haven't had a chance to absorb it.

Generally, any information written on the board or shown on overheads contains major points that you should include in your notes. However, do not stop there. You should also include as much of what the lecturer says as possible. Listen carefully to what the instructor says, paying close attention to cues, sometimes called signal words, that the speaker uses. *Cues* are transitional words that indicate what is coming next and often how important it will be. They are used by a speaker to connect one idea to another. Learn to tune in to cue words to guide you in your note taking. The following chart lists some of these words.

Samples of Cues or Transitional Words and Phrases

There are four parts to . . . first, second, third, fourth, or last . . .

This is important, a major factor, the primary reason, most, often . . .

Next, then, before, after, when . . .

Because, since, consequently, as a result . . .

On the other hand, however, but, nevertheless, meanwhile, yet . . .

For instance, for example . . .

Rarely, sometimes, occasionally, this is an exception, seldom . . .

In addition to listening for cues or signal words, you should be aware of other clues that will help you discover major points. Note when your instructor repeats information. Unless you have an absent-minded professor, *repeated* information should be considered *important* information. Also, pay attention to the speaker's body language. Often the speaker's hand gestures, facial expressions, tone and volume of voice, or other physical movements can signal to you the relative importance of the verbal information.

A legitimate question at this point might be, "Should I write down every word the speaker says?" The answer is, "No, you really can't do that; it's basically impossible." In the first place, unless the speaker talks as slowly as a turtle walks, it would be physically impossible to write down every word. Second, it's not important to take down every word; what is important is the major points and main ideas, with as *many* details as you are able to include. If you fall behind, realize you have missed a point, or cannot write as much as you want, leave space so that you can fill in information after class (see the Edit step).

One way to streamline your note taking is to use abbreviations. Some abbreviations are universal, such as &, =, ?, +, and $, but you need to create your own personal system of abbreviations for every course as well. Often you can anticipate what can be abbreviated when you read your assignment for the day. For example, if you read a chapter on Sigmund Freud's theories for your psychology class, you could abbreviate that phrase as "SFs theories." Take care, however, that you do not get carried away with your abbreviations.

Observe what this student wrote from a lecture on elephants:

Student's notes: "Ls r frm As or Af nd hv ivry tks, lv 60-80 yrs, nd et brs, alf, nd frt n cptvy."

This student's overdone abbreviations stand for "Elephants are from Asia or Africa and have ivory tusks, live 60 to 80 years, and eat berries, alfalfa, and fruit in captivity." The abbreviation certainly saved the student a lot of writing time, but translating it back into words is time-consuming, and it defeats the purpose of note taking. Your goal is to understand your notes at a glance, both now and weeks later.

Some students prefer to take notes in the five-inch column on only *one* side of the page. What might at first seem like a waste of paper really provides you with a way to get the most out of your notes. By leaving the back side of your notes blank, you have room to supplement your notes.

That empty page has all kinds of possibilities:

- Put vocabulary words or terms in the three-inch column and their definitions in the five-inch column.
- Make up your own example(s) to parallel examples that your instructor gave.

- Include charts, diagrams, formulas, or other information to round out your notes.
- Add your own comments and observations.
- Draw pictures to illustrate your notes.
- Write down questions to ask your instructor about information that you do not understand or that you need clarified.

As you use the back side of your notes to enhance them, you will probably come up with even more ways to make this "scratch pad" a useful study aid.

Some students mistakenly believe that a tape recorder can serve as a substitute for taking notes. However, this is completely false. In certain circumstances, using a tape recorder in class might be helpful, but only as a backup for your own notes. For instance, if your instructor speaks very quickly, uses vocabulary that is over your head, or seems to be disorganized, you could use a tape recorder in class to help you clean up or edit your notes after class. Also, if you are taking a foreign language, you might want to tape the lecture to listen to and imitate the pronunciation of words. Finally, in the very rare circumstance when you know ahead of time that you must miss a class, you could ask someone else to tape that lecture for you. Of course, if you do use a tape recorder, you should always get your instructor's permission beforehand.

One more point needs to be made about note taking. As you well know, not all college professors use the lecture method. Many instructors use informal lectures, class discussions, group work, or other methods. It is just as important to take notes at these times as it is when the instructor is speaking. In nonlecture class meetings, the instructor is letting the class discover the information necessary for an understanding of the subject. This is information you will also need when you study for tests. So when a discussion begins or when you are working in a group, do not lay your pen down and close your notebook: *listen, participate, and take notes!*

Step Three: Edit

The third step of GREAT, Edit, is done as soon as possible after class and is simply a clean-up stage. At this time you need to read over your notes to make sure they are clear, legible, and understandable. You may need to fill in missing words, check the spelling of technical words, or clarify abbreviations you used. You might even want to check with your instructor or another student, or consult your textbook, if you missed something in order to fill any "holes" or blank spaces in your notes. During the Edit stage, you should not try to rewrite or type your notes; that would be much too time-consuming. Nor do you need to erase any information. Your goal is to make your notes usable and readable so that you can study them efficiently. Be sure you have numbered and dated each page.

The sooner you Edit after class, the more likely you will be to remember information that you were unable to write down during the class. If possible, the *best* time to Edit is right after class. In any case, try to Edit within the first eight hours after the class, but no later than twenty-four hours.

Step Four: Ask Questions

The fourth step of GREAT, Ask questions, usually follows editing your notes. At this point, you put yourself in the role of teacher and of active

learner to become the questioner. As you read through your notes, you look for chunks of information, ideas that fit together because they are related concepts, such as a main idea with supporting details or examples. Then you view each chunk of information as the answer to an implied question, a question that your teacher is likely to ask you on the next quiz or test. Write that question in the three-inch column of your notebook paper. (See the "Critical Thinking" example on page 16.)

If you want to make a game of the Ask questions step, think of yourself as a contestant on the popular quiz show *Jeopardy*. On that show, contestants are given categories with answers, and it is up to the contestants to give the appropriate questions to match those answers.

In your case, your notes for a day's class are the answers, and your job is to create complete questions for the answers in your notes.

Your questions should be complete sentences, not just phrases or key words. Once you have written a question, you might want to high-light key words in your notes that answer that question. By writing questions, *you* are controlling the information and making your own study guide at the same time.

When you use this method, you are a proactive learner rather than a reactive learner. A *proactive learner* is a learner who is in control of his or her learning. Thus, you are a proactive learner as you analyze the information and write meaningful questions. You are both physically and mentally involved. You are working in a positive framework, anticipating questions that might be asked and the way you might answer them. A *reactive learner,* on the other hand, is a passive learner, someone waiting for something to happen. Such a student might take notes in a class, but thinks that is sufficient. The reactive learner reacts with surprise when quizzes or tests are given, as if the instructor had come up with the questions out of the blue.

When you are writing questions, you need to keep this guideline in mind: The *quality* of questions can be important. The better the quality of a question, the more information your response will include. If you begin your questions with words like "do/does," "can/could," "will/would," or "is/are," the answers they will generate are "yes" or "no." You want to avoid these types of questions. At first, you will have a tendency to write many questions beginning with "what," "who," or "when" because these are the first questions to come to mind. There is certainly nothing wrong with writing these kinds of questions, but you will discover that

Critical Thinking   5/15
                                                                   p.1

How does critic. thinking differ from just thinking?	Thinking = the way we make sense of world → Critical thinking = thinking about how we think ← to clarify and to improve it
Explain the word "critical."	"Kritikos" Greek origin – to question, make sense of, analyze "criticize" = to question, to evaluate (not destructive but constructive)
What are the 5 major components of thinking critically?	Components (5) of critical thinking 1. Thinking actively 2. Exploring situations w. ?s 3. Thinking for ourselves 4. Viewing situations fr. diff. perspectives 5. Discuss ideas in an organized way
Explain 4 elements needed to think actively.	Four elmts to thinking actively: 1. get involved (not on the side-line!) 2. take the initiative (make decisions on yr own) 3. follow thru (when going gets tuff) 4. take respons. for self (re: internal locus of control)
Give examples of the two kinds of outside influences on thinking.	Active and Passive influences Parenting = dictator vs. guide Managers = top down vs. grassroots Jobs = repetitive vs. creative
How does J. Chaffee classify questions?	Exploring situations w ?'s (#2) J. Chaffee's categories are • factual (obj. info.) • interpretive (relate by inferences) • synthesized (put parts together) • analytical (take apart) • evaluative (judge truth. reliability) • appreciative (apply to other situations)

they allow you to answer with only one or two words. Look at the following example:

> **Your question:** "When did the Boston Tea Party occur?"
> **Your answer:** "December 16, 1773."

These so-called *literal questions* will allow you to answer in only a very limited way, with purely factual information. Certainly you will need to know facts, dates, and names, but you will also need to understand relationships and complex material. To prepare yourself for tests that will require this kind of knowledge, you must venture into the realm of *critical-thinking questions.*

A more inclusive question about the same topic could be this:

> **Your question:** "Explain some of the Acts that led to the Boston Tea Party before the Revolutionary War."
> **Your answer:** It should include:

- Naming various Acts passed by the British Parliament
- Describing how these Acts affected the colonies

This example illustrates how much more useful critical-thinking questions are for studying the material. Critical-thinking questions are higher-quality questions that allow you to give in-depth answers showing relationships, such as comparisons, differences, causes, and effects.

Think of the various qualities of questions as building blocks in a pyramid (see the illustration following). The higher you go, the more sophisticated your questions are, and, therefore, the more meaty your answers will be. When you ask higher-order critical-thinking questions like "why" or "how," you will be able to connect facts and ideas into larger explanations. Some of your questions may begin with words like "describe," "explain," or "contrast." These also are called critical-thinking questions because they advance your thinking beyond the simplest and most basic, literal level. At first, generating even literal-level questions may take time and effort, but with practice you will develop the ability to reach an even more sophisticated level of asking questions. You will be able to write both literal and critical-thinking questions comfortably.

One final kind of question at the top of the pyramid invokes the highest order of thinking needed to be creative and inventive, the "what if" or "what would happen if" question. This kind of question, which is also used frequently in business, industrial, and scientific research, can help you *apply* the information you have.

For example, "what if" is the process a scientist, a physician, or an inventor uses to explore unknowns and create solutions. "What if" has helped researchers develop low-fat foods. "What if" has allowed doctors to use DNA information. "What if" has inspired Steven Spielberg to create realistic special effects. Finally, not too many years ago a computer took up the space of a large room, but now, thanks to someone's "what if," a computer can fit nicely in a person's lap. Each year new innovations and improvements occur because of people asking "what if."

"What if" questions usually do not appear in students' notes, but they can be helpful to you as you creatively explore some topics for a more specialized purpose.

Although Asking questions is the fourth step of GREAT, when the instructor asks a question during class, jot it in your three-inch column. The notes that you take during the discussion or lecture, which you will write in the five-inch section, should be the answer to that question. Also, instructors' questions are usually asked because that information will likely appear on tests or quizzes.

Quality Questions Pyramid

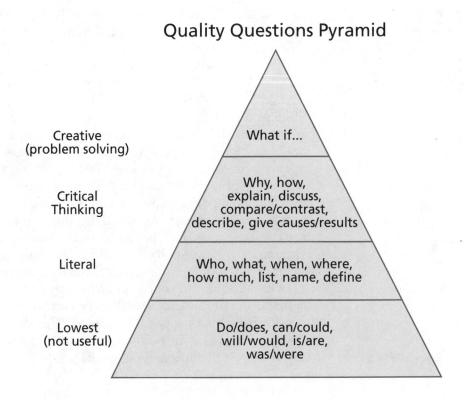

Creative (problem solving) — What if...

Critical Thinking — Why, how, explain, discuss, compare/contrast, describe, give causes/results

Literal — Who, what, when, where, how much, list, name, define

Lowest (not useful) — Do/does, can/could, will/would, is/are, was/were

At the end of the day's lecture notes, you might want to write a *summary statement* or *question* capsulizing the lecture. In order to write a summary statement or question, you should skim your questions in the three-inch margins and write a *big* question that includes all the major points of that day's notes. Such a statement or question is likely to have multiple parts to it, depending on how much information was included in the lecture. You can make this summary stand out by writing all the way across the bottom of the page instead of writing it in the three-inch margin.

For example, in an economics course, after taking notes about where tax revenues come from, you will have written many questions in the three-inch column dealing with various aspects of tax revenue. When you have finished, glance back at your questions and determine how you could summarize the whole day's notes. Your summary question or statement at the bottom of your page might look like this:

> **Summary Statement:** "Describe the five sources of tax revenues (personal income taxes, payroll taxes, sales taxes, property taxes, and corporate income taxes) and explain how each is used."

This summary statement contains the major points from the lecture. Such statements or questions can provide guidelines for studying for comprehensive tests and essay exams.

Step Five: Test Yourself

The "T" in GREAT stands for Test yourself, something that can be done *only* after you have written your questions. In this step, you begin to place information into your long-term memory.

The process is simple. Cover the five-inch column of your notes with a piece of paper or fold over the page, leaving the three-inch column with the questions uncovered. Then read each question and recite—out loud, in your own words—the answer to that question. If you cannot answer a question, study the notes in the main column, then cover them once more, and read the question and recite the answer again. Strive to understand the material. In other words, do not try to memorize what your notes say, but rephrase the information in you own words. Repeat this procedure until you can recite the material without looking at your notes.

Repeated recitation, out loud and in your own words, is the most powerful tool known for placing new information into long-term memory. Think about information you already know. For instance, how did you learn the multiplication tables? By recitation. How did you learn your nine-digit social security number? By repetition.

Reciting *out loud* has a distinct advantage over silent study. You are using *sensory learning*—employing as many senses as possible. By reciting out loud, you are using your sense of hearing in addition to the senses of sight and touch. You use the sense of touch in the act of writing and editing your notes, and you use the sense of sight in reading them. In addition to reciting out loud, you should recite by using your own words. If you do this, you cannot fool yourself into thinking you know the information when you really do not. If you can actually answer your questions meaningfully, that is a good indication that you *understand* the concepts and ideas, and understanding is the basis for all new learning.

The five steps of GREAT—Get ready, wRite, Edit, Ask questions, and Test yourself—will enable you to get the most out of your notes.

Summary

In this chapter, you have been introduced to one of the most powerful tools for succeeding in college: note taking. By examining the Ebbinghaus Forgetting Curve, you have learned that new information is forgotten within a relatively short period of time.

In order to understand what true classroom listening means, you should be aware of the differences between the actions and attitudes of power listeners and passive listeners. Power listeners are those students who are *actively* involved in listening. Passive listeners, on the other hand, do more physical *hearing* than actual mental listening.

Next, the steps of the GREAT note-taking system were explained. GREAT is an acronym for the five steps involved in the note-taking process:

Get ready
wRite
Edit
Ask questions
Test yourself

When you practice these steps, you will see them as a powerful process that allows you to write classroom notes and create a study guide for yourself—all at the same time.

Chapter 2

The Power of Reading for Meaning

"I don't have any trouble reading," the college student said emphatically to his professor. "I just don't know what I've read when I get to the end of the chapter!"

Oops! The logic here seems to be a little off center, to say the least. Sincere as this student may be, the statement about reading does indicate a problem . . . and a big one. Such a statement is like saying, "I don't have any trouble water skiing; I just can't stand up on the skis!" Probably this student is confusing reading for meaning with simply recognizing words. The two are not the same.

In this chapter, you will learn what true reading actually involves, and you will understand why you should adjust your reading speed. In addition, you will distinguish topics from main ideas and recognize differences between major and minor details. You will increase your comprehension by understanding the use of transitions and patterns of organization. Finally, you will discover how to read and interpret visual aids, such as graphs, tables, diagrams, and pictures.

WHAT IS READING?

Some people think that reading means recognizing words. True reading, however, requires thinking and an understanding of the author's message. Certainly, words—just like eyes and good lighting—are necessary reading tools. But more importantly, when you truly engage in the process of reading, you must focus on the *meaning* behind the words in order to understand a writer's ideas. Reading is a process, and a process always involves change: True reading changes words on paper into meaningful thoughts that the reader understands and evaluates.

A good way to illustrate reading for meaning is by comparing three lists like the ones in the exercise below.

Exercise 2-A

Directions: Take a few seconds to look at the following sets of information.

Set 1: s   t   d   k   l   f   r   n   g   p   w

Set 2: far   able   date   high   true   ore   yet   only   from   sort

Set 3: blind   readers   use   their   fingertips   as   tools   for   reading

Which set of information is the easiest for you to recall in the shortest period of time? _____ Why? _____

_____

You probably took only a few seconds to realize that Set 3 is the easiest to recall. Even though it is longer and actually involves more letters, it is the easiest to read because your natural desire to understand makes you cling to the set of letters that makes the most sense!

True reading involves understanding. If you do not already do so, you should read phrase by phrase, not word by word, because this will enable you to grasp the meaning much more easily. For example, compare the two readings of President Lincoln's "Gettysburg Address" written below. Force yourself to pause at each of the slash marks (/) and notice the difference in your reading comprehension.

"Four/ score/ and/ seven/ years/ ago/ our/ fathers/ brought/ forth/ on/ this/ continent/ a/ new/ nation,/ conceived/ in/ liberty/ and/ dedicated/ to/ the/ proposition/ that/ all/ men/ are/ created/ equal."

Stopping after each word makes for jerky reading, doesn't it? Now, read the version below, which is set off phrase by phrase:

> "Four score and seven years ago/ our fathers brought forth on this continent/ a new nation,/ conceived in liberty/ and dedicated to the proposition/ that all men are created equal."

No doubt you can feel and understand Lincoln's message much better in the second version. The first version stops your thoughts at every word; the second one groups your thoughts into meaningful phrases.

ADJUSTING READING TO DIFFERENT PURPOSES

Wherever you go, whatever you do, you are constantly surrounded by printed words. Much of what is written can be read either for enjoyment or for information, and pleasure and learning can even be combined. You need to consider that *what* you are reading and *why* you are reading it determine *how* you should read.

What we read definitely affects *how* we read because we read for many different purposes. For example, would you read a murder mystery the same way you would read a recipe? Would you read an article on exercising the same way you would read a poem? Would you read the information on the sports page of a newspaper the same way you would read the comics? Or, for that matter, would you read the comics the same way you would read a textbook assignment? If you answered any of these questions with a yes, then you may need to learn how to adjust some of your reading habits. If you answered no to all of these questions, then you are well on your way to understanding the various demands of reading.

Reading for Pleasure

When reading for pleasure, you have complete freedom as to how, when, and what you read. You can skip information, skim through the story, or even stop reading if you become bored. For example, when reading a novel full of intrigue and suspense, you might skim through long descriptive passages and just concentrate on the plot. However, when reading about a country that you have never visited, you might slow down to visualize the unfamiliar places and scenes. In contrast, if you are reading a sexy book, you might skim the plot very quickly, but slow down and savor the juicy parts. The point is, when you read just for entertainment, you can read any way you please.

Reading for Information

Newspaper and magazine articles are usually read to obtain general information. The format is very different from that of a novel. Headlines and titles are strategically placed to tempt you to read the whole article. Often, in these types of writing, the first paragraph gives you the most pertinent information—who, what, when, where, and why. Then, depending on your interest in the story, you can decide to read the article completely or skip to another headline that catches your eye.

In contrast to fiction, newspapers, or magazines, a "how to" book or a recipe needs to be read very carefully because you want to make sure

you get all the information you need. Omitting a step or misreading the directions could be disastrous. For example, imagine tasting a cookie made with one *tablespoon* of salt instead of one *teaspoon* because the baker misread the directions. Those would be memorable cookies!

Finally, reading a textbook requires an even more specialized approach. Your primary purpose in reading a textbook is to learn information. However, unlike reading a magazine or a recipe, reading your textbook is usually a mandatory task required to pass most college courses. Thus, you cannot skim your textbook, skip through it, or read it passively. Your goal is to learn as much as you can as efficiently as you can by being an active reader.

The above examples illustrate that your reading is influenced by the type of reading, your purpose, and the printed format. Therefore, the way you read (quickly or slowly, lightly or thoroughly) is determined by whether you are reading for pleasure or for information.

Reading Speed

Students often ask reading teachers, "How fast should I read?" There is no single answer to this question.

Since you are striving for a flexible reading speed with adequate comprehension for your purpose, your speed should depend on *what* you are reading and *why* you are reading it. For example, if you are reading a word problem in math, you may read at fifty to one hundred words per minute, a very slow pace. In contrast, when you first look at your personal mail, you may skim each piece at a thousand words per minute to decide whether you really want to read it or trash it.

Some speed-reading courses promise that their graduates can read at well over a thousand words per minute. Such promises can be misleading because the application of those speeds is very limited. These high speeds are helpful only if you need to skim ten to twenty newspapers per day or if you just want to identify the plots of novels. Speed reading is merely a skimming technique; it can be useful, but it should not be applied to reading textbooks. Your reading speed should always relate to your purpose.

FINDING THE STATED MAIN IDEA IN A PARAGRAPH

At the heart of reading for meaning is the skill of finding the main idea in a paragraph or, more often, in a longer passage. The *main idea* is the major concept the author wants you to understand.

The Paragraph

Think of a good piece of writing as a unified structure, somewhat like a perfectly constructed building. All of the parts of the piece of writing, that is, the paragraphs, fit nicely together and contribute to the whole, again somewhat as in a perfectly constructed building. In a written passage, paragraphs contribute to the whole piece of writing just as rooms contribute to a building's whole structure.

A paragraph usually expresses its own main idea in a sentence, called a topic sentence. The *topic sentence* announces the *topic* or subject of the paragraph and then states the *point* the author wants to make about that topic. A *topic* is simply the person, place, thing, or idea that an author is discussing. It can be expressed in one word or a few words, but it is unfinished all by itself. For example, here is a topic:

the ozone layer

This topic has possibilities, but it doesn't tell you much. By itself, it actually might raise all kinds of questions in your mind. Now, here is that topic expanded into a topic sentence:

The ozone layer [topic] has become dangerously thin, which could threaten all organic life.

If the topic is "the ozone layer," what is the point the author is making? Easy: Organic life may be endangered because of damage done to the ozone layer. Notice that a topic is only a word or a few words, but the topic sentence (because it is the main idea of a paragraph) is always a complete sentence.

A topic sentence may be anywhere in a paragraph—it may be the first sentence, the second, the third, somewhere in the middle, or even the last sentence. Sometimes the thought is actually stated twice. In such

Exercise 2-B

Directions: Take the concept of topic and topic sentence and find the topic sentence in the following paragraph.

Long-distance telephone companies seem to be plotting to keep their customers confused. Several times a week, telephone patrons receive unsolicited calls from representatives of this or that long-distance company offering free long-distance calls for the first so many months, free remote calling cards, free calls to friends and neighbors, free prizes and gifts and rental cars. One company sends checks in the mail for anywhere from $50 to $100; if you endorse the check to spend on anything your heart desires, you have agreed to hook up to the company's long-distance services. The endorsed check is your signed agreement. Some of the ten-cent-per-minute rates actually do apply, but the solicitor fails to mention the fine print: an expensive "switch-over" fee, an "out-of-country-calls-only" clause, and calling at certain times only on the odd days of the even months, or something to that effect.

1. What is the simple topic of this paragraph? _____

_____

2. In your own words, what is the point the author is making about this topic? _____

_____

3. What sentence states this point? _____

_____

a case, the main idea is usually stated in the first sentence and repeated, in different words, in the last sentence.

Most writers want readers to comprehend the message right away, right up front; therefore, they usually make the topic sentence the first or second sentence. You can take advantage of this tendency on the part of writers. For example, you may want to read all first sentences before you thoroughly read an article, which is a method of previewing (see Chapter 3). Furthermore, when you wish to review or summarize information, you might also want to reread first sentences.

Unstated or Implied Main Ideas

Most paragraphs, but not all, contain topic sentences. Sometimes writers do not state the main idea in a sentence; they expect you, the reader, to understand the main idea from the details given. Main ideas that are not stated but are hinted at through the other sentences are called unstated or *implied main ideas*.

Exercise 2-C

Directions: Read the following paragraph, which has an implied main idea, and then answer the following questions.

I followed the line of cars into the parking lot. Before long, I found a parking place. I grabbed my backpack and followed the crowd, walking quickly to the big building on the right. As I entered the doors, I hesitated. "Is this really what I want to do?" I silently asked myself. "Of course," a little voice in my head replied. "Keep moving! You're looking for Room 145." I proceeded down the hall to the last room on the left. As I entered, I could see that most of the desks were occupied, so I had to walk clear over to the windows to find a seat. I looked around, only to see strangers who looked at me with no signs of friendliness. I took a deep breath and tried not to be nervous. I was beginning to get out some paper and a pen from my backpack, when the door opened again. A determined-looking older man with a beard and mustache walked to the front of the room, stood behind the lectern, and said gruffly, "This is Chemistry 101."

1. What is the topic? _____

2. In your own words, what is the point (the implied main idea) the author is making? _____

   _____

3. What would be a good title for this paragraph? _____

   _____

The Main Idea in Longer Readings

Most readings are much longer than a single paragraph, of course. But once you know the structure of the paragraph, you will be able to expand this knowledge to the larger structure of an article, essay, chapter, or book.

The main idea in a longer reading goes by another name, but the basics are the same as in the single paragraph. The main idea in a longer reading is usually called the *thesis* or the *thesis statement.* Just as the topic sentence is usually the first sentence of a paragraph, so, too, the thesis statement is almost always found early in a longer reading. In most essays, for example, the thesis is stated in the first paragraph. Many times, this main idea is repeated in the last paragraph of the essay as well. Knowing this, you would benefit by paying close attention to the first and last paragraphs of an essay, article, or chapter.

MAJOR AND MINOR SUPPORTING DETAILS

You can count on experienced writers to back up or reinforce their main ideas adequately with additional information. These supports or proofs are called supporting details. *Supporting details* include reasons, examples, facts, statistics, definitions, testimonials, and other information that supports or proves the main idea. *Major supporting details* are larger, more general proofs that directly support the main idea. *Minor supporting details* are smaller, more specific bits of information that strengthen the major supporting details. Here is an illustration of the structure of an essay:

Introductory paragraph

Thesis statement

Body Paragraph #1

Topic sentence
Major support #1
minor support
Major support #2
minor support
Major support #3
minor support

Body Paragraph #2

Topic sentence
Major support #1
minor support
Major support #2
minor support
Major support #3
minor support

Body Paragraph #3

Topic sentence
Major support #1
minor support
Major support #2
minor support
Major support #3
minor support

Concluding paragraph

Of course, not all essays are the same length as this example. Essays can be of any length. This diagram simply illustrates how the major supporting details and minor supporting details develop the topic sentences. The topic sentence of each paragraph, in turn, develops one aspect of the thesis statement, the main idea of the essay.

The following paragraph is taken from an economics textbook. This paragraph explains one aspect of gross domestic product (GDP). The first two sentences are introductory sentences. The topic sentence is in bold print, and the major supporting details are underlined. The remaining sentences are minor supporting details used to back up the major supporting details.

The *market value* of final goods and services is their value at market price. The process of determining market value is straightforward where prices are known and transactions are observable. **However, there are cases where prices are not known and transactions are not observable.** For instance, illegal drug transactions are not reported to the government, which means they are not included in gross domestic product (GDP) statistics. In fact, almost any activity that is not traded in a market is not included. For example, production that takes place in households is not counted . . . , nor are unreported barter and cash transactions. For instance, if a lawyer has a sick dog and a veterinarian needs some legal advice, by trading services and not reporting the activity to the tax authorities, each can avoid taxation on the income that would have been reported had they sold their services to each other.

(Boyes & Melvin 139)

Transitions Connecting Ideas

Another way to promote good reading comprehension is to develop an awareness of transitional words. *Transitions* are words that connect one idea to another. Transitions show relationships between ideas. They may be small, but they are extremely powerful words that help you distinguish between main ideas, major supporting details, and minor supporting details.

The following are examples of the most common types of transitions:

1. Transitions that show *additional* information:

first, second, third	next
also	furthermore
another	finally
in addition	moreover

2. Transitions that show *time* relationships:

first	before
next	after
later	until
then	during
often	when
while	meanwhile

3. Transitions that show *comparison* or *sameness:*

just like	equal
like	equally
alike	in the same way
likewise	almost identical to
similar to	comparable to
similarly	the same as

4. Transitions that show *contrast* or *differences:*

in contrast	although
on the other hand	even though, even if
however	yet
but	instead
differ	unlike
different from	despite

5. Transitions that show that *examples* will follow:

for example	including
for instance	such as
to illustrate	one such

6. Transitions that explain *why* or *cause and effect:*

because	the result of
since	as a result
reasons for	therefore
is caused by	thus
if . . . then	so

So, how can these transitional groupings help you read for meaning? The answer is simple: As you become aware of transitional connectors, you should become aware of your powers of prediction. Transitions help you follow a writer's train of thought and predict what he or she will say next.

Exercise 2-D

Directions: Read each of the following unfinished sentences, and predict an ending by finishing the statement. Then circle the most important transitional word and identify what type of transition it is. The first one has been done for you.

1. "My sister and I have a lot in common; (however),
   <u>we definitely disagree on anything related to politics.</u>"

   Kind of transition: *Contrast*

2. "To open a new document on the computer, first, click on the icon called "'Microsoft Office' . . . " _____

   Kind of transition: _____

3. "The doctor said the man was a heart attack waiting to happen. I know, for example, that he smoked too much, ate mostly junk foods, and . . . " _____

   Kind of transition: _____

4. "While I was playing golf, the thunder and lightning began. As a result, . . . " _____

   Kind of transition: _____

5. "The feeling I experience when I get an A on a test is just like . . ." _____

   Kind of transition: _____

6. "The new sporting goods store that opened last week has a wide variety of items for young children, including . . . " _____

   Kind of transition: _____

As you discovered from doing Exercise 2-D, using transitions to predict what is coming can help make you comfortable and confident with your reading. You can also better understand how major and minor supporting details fit together.

Patterns to Show an Author's Organization

So far, you have examined transitions within sentences. In addition, you will find it useful to be able to recognize transitions when they link a sentence to another sentence or a paragraph to another paragraph.

When certain types of transitions are repeated within a paragraph, you are seeing what is called a *pattern of organization*. In this sense, a pattern means a repetition of something. Patterns of organization occur when a writer uses several transitions from one category (addition, time, contrast, comparison, example, or cause and effect). Although patterns of organization are not always present, when they do exist, they are a powerful means of enhancing your comprehension.

Patterns of organization can easily be recognized once you understand transitions. Below you will find some common patterns of organization that are based upon the types of transitions you saw earlier.

Listing Patterns   Listing patterns occur when an author uses addition transitions (first, second, also, in addition, moreover, etc.) to list details in any order the author chooses. The following is an example of a paragraph using the listing pattern of organization. The addition transitions that create this pattern are underlined.

IMPROVING CONCENTRATION

If you have trouble concentrating when you study, you may want to try some of the following suggestions. First, make sure you are not hungry or sleepy or wearing uncomfortable clothes. Another way to keep focused is to eliminate external distractors. You should turn off the radio or television and take the phone off the hook or turn on the answering machine. Next, study at your "peak time," when you are most mentally and physically alert. In addition, make sure your study area is organized, fully equipped, well lighted, and comfortable in terms of temperature. Also, study your hardest or least enjoyable subject first, and take short breaks when your concentration begins to lag. Moreover, plan to reward yourself when you finish a task. These are just a few of the many ways to improve your concentration.

Time Order Patterns   Time order occurs when an author is setting up steps or stages in a process or is describing chronological events. The steps, stages, or events are fixed in a certain order (first, second, then, next, finally, etc.). The following is an example of a paragraph using time order as its pattern of organization. The time transitions that create this pattern are underlined.

HUMAN GROWTH

Once human beings are born, they go through six rather obvious and important stages. <u>First</u>, newborn babies begin to adapt to the external world in the first two weeks of life. <u>Then</u>, as infants up to about fifteen months, babies grow considerably in both height and weight. <u>Next</u>, as children, bone formation and overall growth continue. This lasts up to the age of twelve or so. Puberty begins for girls between twelve and fifteen and for boys between thirteen and sixteen, <u>during which time</u> secondary sexual characteristics develop. Adolescence follows puberty. <u>At this time</u> teenagers mature physically, mentally, and emotionally. <u>The final stage</u> in human growth is adulthood. Between the ages of eighteen and twenty-five, bone formation and growth come to a stop. <u>After that</u>, any changes in adults occur very slowly.

Comparison and Contrast Patterns   Comparison and contrast patterns occur when an author uses comparison (similarly, like, likewise, etc.) and contrast (in contrast, on the other hand, but, etc.) to show how two or more subjects are similar and/or different. The following is an example of a paragraph using the contrast pattern of organization. The contrast transitions that create the pattern of organization are underlined.

THE CREDIT CARD VS. THE DEBIT CARD

Many banks are offering a new kind of plastic card: the debit card. This card goes by various names, but it is essentially the <u>opposite of</u> a credit card. When you use a credit card, you make the purchase at one moment but are billed later, usually within a month. <u>On the other hand</u>, when you use the debit card, your payment is immediate because a computer approves immediate withdrawal from your checking account. Credit cards have an approved charge limit, up to say $3,000 or $10,000 depending upon your spending and credit history. Should you try to charge more than that amount, your credit will not be approved by the card issuer, and you will go home empty-handed. Also, if you do not pay the full amount due each month, interest of roughly 12 to 20 percent will be charged on the balance. <u>In contrast</u>, debit cards have the limit of your own bank account balance. Should you go over that amount, you may have to pay a penalty for overdrawing your account. A final <u>difference</u> lies in bargaining power or guaranteed satisfaction. If you charge on a credit card and something is wrong with the merchandise, you can withhold payment from the store and explain this in writing to the credit card company. Your payment is deferred until the situation is settled. <u>In contrast</u>, with the debit card, your bill is completely paid and you have no leverage for complaining.

Cause-and-Effect Patterns   Cause-and-effect patterns occur when an author uses cause-and-effect transitions (because, as a result, resulting in, etc.) to show how one event leads to another. The following is an example of a paragraph that uses a cause-and-effect pattern of organization. The cause-and-effect words that create this pattern are underlined.

BEING LATE TO CLASS

Being consistently late to class can <u>cause</u> several unpleasant <u>results</u> for you and for others. <u>If</u> you arrive late, <u>then</u> the <u>consequence</u> could be that you miss a quiz or miss hearing about a change of assignments. You might also feel disoriented <u>because</u> you walked in on the middle of a lecture. In addition, your late arrival disturbs the rest of the class. <u>Because</u> they look at you instead of listening to the instructor, you have momentarily made some students lose their concentration. You might even make the instructor lose his or her train of thought. The <u>resultant</u> scowl on the instructor's face indicates a reaction of anger and frustration. In the long run, the <u>result</u> of habitual lateness is a clear demonstration that you lack respect for both your peers and the professor.

Definition-Example Patterns   Definition-example patterns occur when an author defines a term and then explains it through examples or illustrations (for example, for instance, to illustrate, including, such as, one such). The following paragraph illustrates a definition-example pattern of organization. The transitions that indicate examples are underlined.

CLICHÉS IN WRITING

Clichés are phrases or sentences in writing that are overused or trite [definition]. Often they are comparisons (similes) that were clever the first time they were used, but have been repeated so many times that they have lost their freshness. <u>For instance</u>, some common clichés refer to varying degrees of heat or cold, such as "cold as ice," "hot as Hades," "cool as a cucumber," or "warm as toast." <u>Other examples</u> of clichés include "pretty as a picture," "red as a rose," "big as a house," or "dead as a doornail." <u>To illustrate</u> how easy it is to come up with clichés, finish these sentences with the first words that pop into your mind: "I'm so hungry I could eat a _____." "The child was as quiet as a _____." "He was faster than a _____." Chances are, your responses were "cow," "mouse," and "speeding bullet," or similarly trite words. Good writers avoid clichés and create new, bright images of their own as they write.

In conclusion, as you saw previously, transitions can help you understand and predict what is coming in a sentence. When transitions are repeated into patterns of organization, you can understand and predict an author's message in a paragraph or an essay. Often main ideas seem to stand out more readily when details settle themselves into recognizable patterns.

READING VISUAL AIDS

College textbooks, and many magazines and newspapers as well, contain not only printed information, but also *visual aids,* such as graphs, tables, diagrams, and pictures. These visual aids are not simply page decorations, something you can skip. The general purposes of visual aids are to explain processes, condense detailed information, compare related ideas, show change over time, or otherwise support the text.

You would do well to follow some general guidelines in order to understand visual aids. Here are some helpful tips:

- Get an overview of the entire visual aid by observing the printed title, caption, units of measurement, terms used, years covered, etc. You want to get an overview of the visual aid.

- Now carefully read all printed information. This may include what is called a legend. A *legend* is an explanatory caption, table, list, or chart found on or next to the visual aid. The legend gives information that helps you interpret the meaning of the visual aid.
- Next, carefully study the actual visual aid for details.
- Try to see what relationships exist between the words and pictures.
- To check your understanding of the visual aid, try to summarize the information in a few sentences.

Reading Graphs

Graphs are visual aids that show comparisons and/or contrasts between two or more items. Three popular types of graphs often used in textbooks are line graphs, bar graphs, and pie graphs.

Line graphs are visual aids in which information is plotted using horizontal and vertical axes. The major use of a line graph is to show changes over time and/or trends. The following is a line graph plotting the amount of information a person retains over periods of time:

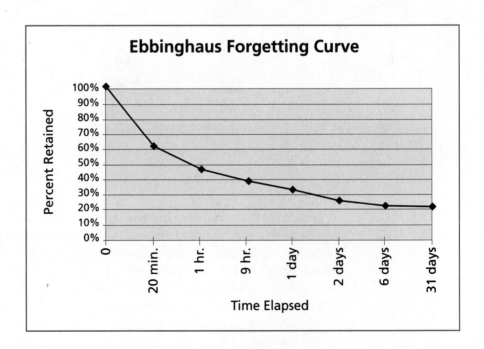

To read a line graph, take a point on the line, and trace down to the information on the horizontal axis and across to the information on the vertical axis. This will tell you how the two variables are related (in this case, the time elapsed and percent retained). Two pieces of paper, or other straightedges, placed across the two directions may help you clearly see the point of intersection.

Bar graphs are graphs that use thick lines, or bars of various lengths, arranged either horizontally or vertically, to show comparisons among quantities or amounts. Sometimes bar graphs are stacked; that is, the whole concept being examined is broken into its various parts. Often different colors or shadings are used to represent these different parts of the larger category. The following is an example of a bar graph:

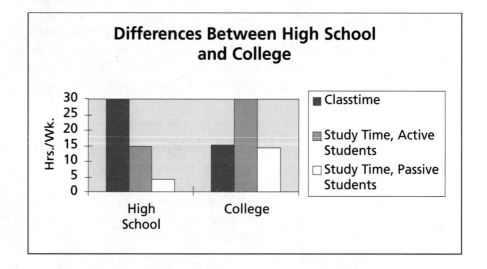

To understand bar graphs, first read the title and any explanation given in order to understand the main idea behind the bar graph. Then look at the vertical and horizontal labels to determine what is being measured and the units of measurement. In the above example, for instance, the legend to the right indicates what the shaded bars represent. With this information in mind, you can see how each bar is related to hours per week. Then you can compare and contrast the different uses of learning time among high school and college students. Using a piece of paper or a ruler for a guide, you can look at the value in the horizontal column and see where it intersects with the vertical column. That intersection tells you how the two relate to each other.

Pie graphs or circle graphs, unlike the other two types of graphs, are in the shape of a circle. Each slice of the circle or pie represents a percentage, with the whole pie representing 100 percent. Pie graphs quickly show you how each part relates to the whole. The following graph shows the percentage of time one student spends on each activity during a typical school week:

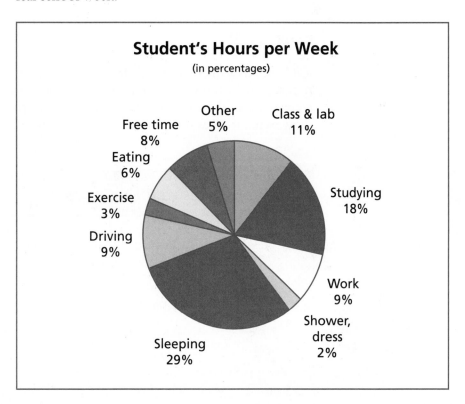

To read a pie graph, you simply see how large each slice of the pie is (what percentage) compared to the whole pie (100 percent). In the case of the student above, the percentages represent this much time during a week (168 hours):

Class & lab	11 percent	=	18 hours
Studying	18 percent	=	30 hours
Work	9 percent	=	15 hours
Shower, dress	2 percent	=	4 hours
Sleeping	29 percent	=	50 hours
Driving	9 percent	=	15 hours
Exercise	3 percent	=	5 hours

Eating	6 percent	=	10 hours
Free time	8 percent	=	13 hours
Other	5 percent	=	8 hours

When you read any pie graph, the larger the pie slice, the more value, time, or weight an item represents.

Reading Tables

Tables are lists of percentages, facts, numbers, or other related information set up in rows and columns. This arrangement allows you to see comparisons easily. The following table, taken from a biology textbook, shows what it takes to burn calories from four different foods:

What It Takes to Burn Calories

Food	Activity	Calories/ minute	Time to Burn (minutes)
Milkshake	Resting	1.1	289
318 Calories	Walking	5.5	58
	Swimming	10.9	29
	Running	14.7	22
Corn, 2 pats	Resting	1.1	155
butter	Walking	5.5	31
170 Calories	Swimming	10.9	16
	Running	14.7	12
Corn,	Resting	1.1	63
unbuttered	Walking	5.5	13
70 Calories	Swimming	10.9	6
	Running	14.7	5

(Levine & Miller 738)

To understand a table, first read the general title in order to find out what is the subject under discussion, in this case "What It Takes to Burn Calories." Then read the labels at the tops of the columns; these will tell you how the subject was broken down for analysis. In this table, the labels are "Food," "Activity," "Calories/minute," and "Time to Burn (minutes)." Next, read the descriptive information under the labels from left to right. You may want to use a ruler or a piece of paper under each line of information in order to keep your eyes accurately focused as you read across the line.

Reading Diagrams

Diagrams include drawings or illustrations used to represent processes, ideas, the operations or working parts of a physical object, a system of the human body, plans for the future, or any other such information. The following diagram illustrates the parts of the human eye:

Human eye

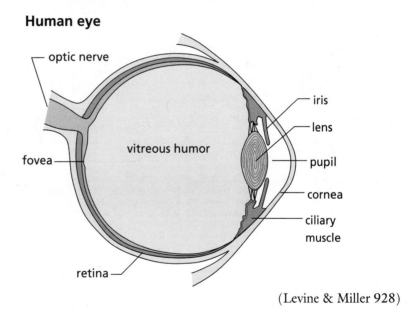

(Levine & Miller 928)

To read a diagram, look at the title or heading first. Then read the labels and view the pictures to get an overall idea of what is represented in the diagram. Next, study the diagram, trying to see how each part fits into the whole picture or system. For instance, in studying the diagram of the human eye, you will want to know the parts of the eye and their location. You may also need to know the function of each part. If the diagram is one you will have to reproduce or label on an exam, one way to study it is to trace it and try to label your tracing with the names of the parts. Then you can compare your reproduction with the one in the text to check your accuracy. Another way to study a diagram is to mark the textbook diagram by inserting the particular function of each part.

Another type of diagram is called a flow chart. A *flow chart* shows step-by-step procedures or the top-to-bottom line of command in an organization. Diagrams of this type are usually read from top to bottom, although at times they are set up to be read from left to right. Connecting lines and arrows usually guide you as you move through the process. Often boxes or circles represent the stages or steps in the process. The following flow chart, which is read from top to bottom, shows the functional divisions of the human nervous system:

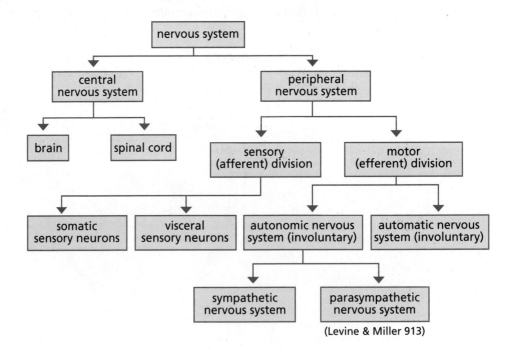

(Levine & Miller 913)

Observing Photographs and Pictures

One more category of visual aids that you will encounter in textbooks is photographs, pictures, and cartoons. The general guidelines for reading and understanding these visual aids are similar to those for graphs, tables, and diagrams: Get an overview, read the printed details (if any), and study the picture details. However, with a photograph, picture, or cartoon, your main goal is to understand the picture, connect it to your experience, and draw a conclusion about it in relation to the subject you are studying. Your conclusions are drawn from your observations of the picture itself within the context of the chapter, as well as your own background and logic. In this sense, understanding pictures is more personal and less exact than interpreting graphs, tables, and diagrams.

Summary

In this chapter, you learned how reading, by definition, requires that you read for meaning. Because reading is an individual and unique process, your approaches to reading and reading rates must be adjusted to accommodate varying purposes and types of reading materials.

You also learned how to recognize main ideas, which are the topic sentences of paragraphs and thesis statements of essays. These main ideas can be stated or implied. In addition, you examined major and minor supporting details and the importance of recognizing transitions. Transitional words link sentences to sentences and paragraphs to paragraphs, and they create patterns of organization within a paragraph.

Finally, you discovered ways to read and understand visual aids, which include graphs, tables, diagrams, and pictures.

Chapter 3

The Power of STUDY-READING

Remember your first-grade reading lessons? "See Dick run. See Jane run. See Spot run." Why bother to examine the power of reading at the college level, since reading comes second nature to you now? You outgrew Dick and Jane and Spot a long time ago, but have you grown beyond simple reading practices to more demanding and sophisticated ones? Your reading skills now need to be adjusted to your appropriate level of learning as an active college student.

In this chapter, you will first learn how to examine your textbooks at the beginning of each course to familiarize yourself with the contents. Next, you will learn a powerful way to make your textbooks work for you: using the STUDY-READ method. This method will allow you to turn your textbooks into personal study guides.

EXAMINING AN ENTIRE TEXTBOOK

Before beginning the intense reading of individual text chapters, you need to get an initial overview of each textbook. That is, at the beginning of each term, you need to examine all your textbooks. This means much more than just thumbing through each book to see how many pages it has and if there are any pictures. Surveying or previewing a textbook is a way to make yourself familiar with it, to see where you are going before you get there, to understand the parts and the whole. Most instructors never mention the various aspects of the textbooks they use, but they expect you to take the initiative to investigate what your text contains so that you can use all of its resources. The more you know about the text before you start any class, the easier it will be for you to read each chapter and to understand how it will fit into the entire course.

In examining a textbook, look at the following features:

- Title (on the cover and the title page)
- Publication date (on the reverse side of the title page)
- Edition (on the cover and the title page)
- Author(s)
- Foreword, Introduction, or To the Student
- Table of Contents
- Index
- Appendix(es) (at back of book)
- Glossary (at back of book or end of chapters)
- Answer key
- Additional information (keys, charts, lists) on inside covers

These features will be found in most college textbooks. A quick survey of all your textbooks will provide you with an understanding of the features of each of them.

Examining your textbooks gives you an opportunity to learn about your courses and helps you understand what you will be expected to know. During your survey, you may have discovered that the text was written by a very distinguished person in that particular field of study, maybe even your own instructor. The date of publication and the edition tell you how recently the book was printed or revised. If it is a revised edition, the foreword or introduction will usually tell you how the book has been improved or updated as well as explain the major purposes or concepts of the text.

By looking at the table of contents, you will gain an overview of what material is included in the text and how the information is organized. The chapter titles should indicate whether the information will be familiar to you or not. The subheadings for each chapter give you an outline of the chapter itself. In addition, some books are divided not just into chapters, but into larger sections or parts. These larger units provide you with an understanding of the major divisions of the text.

Investigating information contained in each of your textbooks will familiarize you with all of their resources. Appendixes, glossaries, answer keys, and charts on the inside covers of the text provide you with quick ways to find information. Knowing all the special aspects of each of your textbooks gives you the power to use them wisely.

Exercise 3-A

Directions: This exercise shows you how to examine a textbook. Answer all the questions as they relate to this study skills book.

1. What is the title? (Look at the cover or the title page.) _____

   _____

2. When was it published? (See the reverse side of the title page.) _____ What edition is it?_____

3. Name the author(s). _____

4. Read the introduction. State one important fact that you learned from this section._____

   _____

5. Next look at the table of contents. How many chapters are listed?

   _____

6. Do most of the chapter titles look familiar? Yes _____ No_____

7. Does the book have an index at the back? Yes _____ No_____

8. From your preliminary preview, do you think this will be an easy text to read or a difficult one? _____ Give a reason for your answer. _____

   _____

READING A TEXTBOOK CHAPTER: STUDY-READ

Have you ever finished an assignment, congratulated yourself for being done, and realized that you don't remember a word of what you just read? Have you ever been so bored you thought you would never finish? Have you ever actually fallen asleep while trying to read an assignment? How frustrating those experiences are, and how terribly time-consuming it is to reread the entire assignment. You might, on the other hand, read the assignment and think you know what it is all about, but when you take quizzes, you get only Cs. By midterm, you are not doing as well as someone else who seems to put in less time than you do.

If you fall into one of these categories or for some other reason are not achieving the grades you want on quizzes and tests covering textbook content, you need to develop a more effective method of completing your reading assignments. You need STUDY-READ.

STUDY-READ, a process for reading and studying textbook chapters, consists of three parts:

- Preview
- Read and mark
- Review by reciting

This system evolved from two sources: the learning theories of experts in the college study skills field and the actual study habits of successful students.

By using STUDY-READ, you can become a more active reader, instead of a passive reader. Active readers use *sensory learning,* engaging as many of their senses as they can—sight, sound, touch—as they study in order to understand and remember the information. They are thinking about what they are reading and trying to make ideas and concepts meaningful. Active readers, by reading for meaning and understanding, are making their study time worthwhile. Passive readers often only go through the motions of reading without really grasping the meaning; the words just travel in front of their eyes.

With a little effort and practice, STUDY-READ will provide you with a new habit that will make learning easier and more enjoyable. You will be putting in quality time and getting quality results. The rewards you will gain will include a much better understanding of the material and, most likely, better grades. Using STUDY-READ will make you feel as though you have been to a two-for-one sale: You will read with depth and understanding, and you will create your own study guides at the same time. Once you master the system, it will make preparing for classes and exams easier and more effective.

The three parts of STUDY-READ—preview, read and mark, and review by reciting—are all integral to the system, although they are performed separately. The following diagram presents an overview of the STUDY-READ method. At the center of the STUDY-READ process is the familiar activity of reading, combined with text marking. In this system, reading is preceded by the mental warm-up of previewing; thus the arrow is pointing toward the reading. Once you have read and marked your chapter, your final step is to review by reciting; thus the arrow points back to the read and mark stage. Reviewing allows you to store information in your long-term memory and later retrieve it.

Step 1: PREVIEW ➡

Previewing or surveying the chapter is the first step in STUDY-READ; it provides your brain with a systematic overview of the new information discussed in the chapter. Just as you examined or previewed your whole textbook, now you will take a close survey of the chapter.

1. First, read the *title* of the chapter to determine what clues the title provides to predict the chapter content.
2. Next, if the chapter begins with an *introduction* or *chapter objectives*, read them.
3. Then, quickly thumb through the chapter and read all *boldfaced headings*; they will give you an outline of the main ideas of the chapter. If your textbook has no boldfaced headings, you can skim the first sentence of the larger paragraphs. Since the first sentence is often a topic sentence, it may act as a substitute for a boldfaced heading.
4. Another item to notice as you preview the chapter is all *nonverbal information*. This includes maps, charts, graphs, diagrams, pictures, and cartoons. As you examine these visual aids, read any captions that accompany them.
5. When you reach the end of the chapter, read the *summary* or *conclusion* if there is one.
6. Finally, if the chapter ends with *questions*, read them. End-of-chapter questions are usually sequential, so reading them will give you an added picture of the organization of the chapter as well as a summation of what the author thinks is important.

Exercise 3-B

Directions: Preview the next chapter you will be reading in this text, timing yourself as you do so. Then answer the following questions without referring back to that chapter.

1. How long did it take you to preview the chapter? _____

2. What are the *major* points in the chapter?

   _____

3. What information seems familiar? _____

   _____

   _____

4. What information seems new? _____

   _____

   _____

(continued on the next page)

Exercise 3-B (continued)

5. What is another feature, idea, or aspect of the chapter that you
   noticed? _____

   _____

Reading and understanding the explanation of the six steps in pre-viewing a chapter probably took you longer than actually doing a pre-view. In fact, it should take you approximately five or, at the most, ten minutes to preview your assignment.

The few minutes it takes to preview a chapter are a good investment of time. Looking over the chapter as you preview helps you understand the organization of the material. This will greatly increase your compre-hension and will also make your reading easier.

The short time spent in surveying definitely pays for itself. Once you begin to preview all your reading assignments and adopt previewing as a habit, the task will become easier and easier. Previewing is just the begin-ning of STUDY-READ, but it adds extra power to activate the next step.

Step 2: READ and MARK

The second step in STUDY-READ is actually reading the textbook chapter, and reading it in such a way that you are systematically and ac-tively engaged in learning. Reading merely to finish the chapter and reading to understand the material are two entirely different approaches to reading. The first way will leave you dissatisfied because you will re-member very little of what you have read. The second way, reading to understand and marking the text as you read, will leave you with a feel-ing of accomplishment and a good start on remembering what you have read because you are actively involved in the reading. After all, textboook reading is intense reading for knowledge and understanding.

In step 2 of STUDY-READ, called the read-and-mark step, you will read each paragraph or each section set off by a boldface heading, one at a time. Your goal is to find the main idea, which is usually the topic sentence, and then find the supporting details, facts, reasons, or examples. You are actively reading with an inquiring, questioning mind. What is the major point? What details support this point? You are reading to find answers.

To begin the read-and-mark step of STUDY-READ, you should

read one whole paragraph or section completely *before* marking. Ultimately, you need to determine what question(s) the material in the paragraph answers. Determine your questions by second-guessing what your instructor might ask in a class discussion, on a quiz, or on a test or final exam. Make your questions complete sentences that cannot be answered with yes or no. Use questions like "what," "when," or "how much," but strive for higher-order questions like "how" and "why," as well as comparisons, contrasts, and explanations. Just as you want good questions in your notes, you want to strive for quality questions in your textbooks (see the Quality Questions Pyramid in Chapter 1).

Then for each paragraph or, at most, each section, actually write your question(s) in the margin of your text and mark, by highlighting or underlining, key words or phrases that will answer your question(s). The rule of thumb when highlighting is "less is more." In other words, be very selective about what you highlight. Novice or beginning highlighters tend to overkill by highlighting whole paragraphs and whole pages. Such textbook pages are colorful, but they are not very useful when it comes time to study.

Besides writing questions, you may also need or want to add other marginal notes—numbers 1, 2, 3, etc., for lists of items, stars (*) for very important information, def. for definitions, and ex. for examples. Marking your textbook makes it a working tool for you.

Complete this read-and-mark step for a paragraph or section before you go on to the next paragraph or section. Then follow the same procedure for the next paragraph or section, and the next, and the next. As you go along, you are creating a series of questions in the margins of your book, with key words highlighted as answers to those questions. You will know what you have read, and you will be more likely to be ready to take tests.

Note: For an example of a textbook page illustrating the read-and-mark step of STUDY-READ, see the example "Understanding the Art of Concentration" (Patterson 17–18) in this chapter.

When you have completed the whole reading assignment or chapter, challenge yourself to write one more question or statement at the end of the chapter: a summary of the whole chapter. Granted, writing a summary question may seem difficult at first, but it will help you put the parts back into the whole and give you an overview of the chapter. (See Chapter 1 for more information about summary questions or statements.)

Here is an example of a summary question based on the information in the "Art of Concentration" excerpt:

> **Summary Question:** "Name the three mental abilities necessary for concentration and tell how they affect each other."

By using the physical and mental process of actively reading and marking a textbook, you are being a proactive learner rather than being a reactive learner who passively reads the assignment sentence by sentence, just trying to finish.

The proactive learner using read and mark will discover that this method has many advantages:

- By deriving questions from the answers that are already there (i.e., the text itself), you keep your mind actively on your reading and avoid daydreaming.
- By writing the questions and marking key words, you are using sensory learning, engaging your senses of sight and touch in the process of reading and learning.
- By marking, you are actively creating your own study guide.
- By reading and marking, you may spare yourself having to reread *all* of the material when you review.
- By using this method, you can easily take a break at any point instead of doing the entire reading at one sitting. If you have marked your text and written questions, it is easy to find your place to continue when you return to the assignment.

UNDERSTANDING THE ART OF CONCENTRATION

MENTAL ABILITIES

What 3 mental abilities are involved in concentration?

Concentration involves a series of three mental abilities: ① the ability to sustain <u>focus over a period of time,</u> ② the ability to <u>focus at will</u> and ③ the ability to <u>focus on one task at a time</u>. These three separate abilities each need to be explained, but since they work together, they need to be considered as an interactive and connected whole.

Sustaining Focus Over a Period of Time

The first mental ability is sustaining focus over a period of time. Do you have trouble settling down with a complex problem because your mind keeps shifting to another topic? Do you start a conversation with a friend, then remember the math problems that are due the next day? As soon as the math problems are started, do you decide to take the dog for a walk? Are you usually busy but don't seem to get that much accomplished?

How long can a typical student concentrate?

For challenging or <u>difficult mental tasks</u> (which include much of college work), the optimum concentration <u>span is 10 to 50 minutes</u>. In one study, college students reported concentration spans from 1 to 105 minutes with an average concentration span of 16 minutes for textbooks (Patterson, 1993). The implications of this study are that <u>15-20 minute study periods enable us to read</u> in a textbook <u>with maximum concentration</u>.

How can I vary my studies and increase concentration?

Instead of giving up studies when your mind wanders, however, try <u>breaking up</u> your <u>study</u> periods <u>with a variety of activities</u> so you can <u>sustain focus over a longer period of time</u>. For example, Mike, an Emergency Medical Technician student, tries to concentrate on an anatomy text but finds his eyes looking at words without really understanding, even though he's just two hours into an eight hour study day. He could vary the task by <u>reading for 20 minutes</u>, <u>studying anatomy charts for the next 20 minutes,</u> and <u>testing</u> himself over <u>what he's read for the next 20 minutes</u>.

<u>A short break</u> will also <u>keep concentration to a maximum</u>. Mike's concentration will be better if he sets 20 minute study goals and <u>intersperses</u> these <u>study periods with a relaxation exercise,</u> an <u>eye break</u> which consists of focusing on something in the distance, or a <u>short aerobic workout</u>. Taking a short break every hour gives him the energy he needs to sustain focus for longer periods of time.

What other factors influence my focus-over-time abilities?

Give examples.

The ability to <u>sustain focus depends</u> on both your ①<u>motivation</u> and on the ②<u>task</u>. Concentration spans vary according to people's motivation to do the task. Those who are <u>highly motivated may maintain focus for hours</u> at a time. Learning to motivate yourself, thus, becomes an important ability, enabling you to increase your concentration span. Concentration spans also vary according to the task. If you are <u>working at the computer</u>, you may <u>pay attention for three hours</u>, yet a <u>difficult physics textbook</u> may only keep your <u>full attention for five minutes</u>. Some of my students reported better concentration in difficult material because the text was challenging, they couldn't let their minds wander at all. One goal of this book is to increase your amount of sustained concentration by increasing your motivation and learning how to concentrate in a variety of tasks.

Focusing at Will

Explain the signs of a person who cannot "Focus at Will."

A second concentration skill is the <u>ability to "focus at will" rather than being at the mercy of interest</u> or a good <u>mood</u>. Jennifer is a college junior who gets good grades but suffers from a series of <u>stress-related illnesses</u>. She needs advice about how to concentrate on a school paper when it is assigned rather than <u>waiting to write</u> it the <u>night before it is due</u>. She <u>isn't</u> in the <u>right mood to write</u> on Monday, Tuesday, or Wednesday, and has to stay up all Thursday night in order to turn the paper in on Friday. Are you like Jennifer?

When you have finished this step, you have provided yourself with an easy way to review your material.

Step 3: ⬅ REVIEW by RECITING

Once you have finished reading and marking the chapter assigned, you are ready to complete the learning process by transferring the information into your long-term memory. This third step in STUDY-READ is called *review by reciting*. As the arrow in the heading above indicates, you will be going back to the questions in your text and reciting the marked information. As you review, you will be able to determine what you know and what you need to review in more depth. This step allows your long-term memory to retain the valuable answers you have marked in step 2. Your recitation should be done aloud so that you use sensory learning—engaging your sense of hearing, along with your senses of sight and touch.

To accomplish this last step, review by reciting, return to the beginning of the chapter, and cover the text with a piece of paper or gently fold the page over to cover everything except your questions. Look at the questions you have written in the margins and recite the answers aloud, in your own words. Do this as soon as you finish reading and marking the chapter, while the answers are still fresh in your mind. If you mark your chapter without the follow-up recitation, you are likely to *think* you know the answers, but when you have to take a test, you may not *remember* the information.

Next, check the accuracy and thoroughness of your recited answer by looking at the key words or phrases you marked. If you are unable to answer your own question, then you need to look at the answer once more and recite aloud again, or even do this several times. This review-by-reciting step should be done as often as necessary until you feel confident that you know all the material.

An Alternative: Using Summary Paper

If you have borrowed a book or magazine or are using one from the library, of course you should not write in it. That does not mean, however, that you cannot use the read-and-mark step of STUDY-READ. Also, some people feel that they learn better when they write down information. In either case, you can follow the STUDY-READ method, but instead of marking the textbook, use your summary paper just as if you were taking notes.

On your summary paper, first title the page with the subject of the reading assignment and any other pertinent information you might need, such as the title of the book, the author(s), the publication date, the edition, and so on. You need to title only the first page of a group of pages of your notebook that are all from the same source. See the following example:

Ch. 4 (pp. 64–84), "Growth and Diversity, 1720–1770," in *A People & a Nation: A History of the US*. Brief, 4th ed. Vol. A, by Mary Beth Norton, et al., pub. Houghton Mifflin (Boston), 1996.	
Write your	Write the
questions	key-word answers
in the three-inch margin.	in the five-inch column.

Then, after previewing the assignment, as you read each paragraph or section, write your questions in the three-inch margin, and write your key-word answers in the five-inch column. You should include the page number(s) for each key-word answer in case you need to go back to your source later for more information.

Exercise 3-C

Directions: Now that you have read about STUDY-READ, begin writing questions and highlighting or underlining each paragraph or section from this point on. (Feel free to return to previous reading assignments to read and mark your texts so that you can review by reciting.)

STUDY-READ IN VARIOUS DISCIPLINES

The STUDY-READ method is the most effective way to read your text-books, but sometimes different types of textbooks or assignments require changes or refinements in the process. Following are some points you should consider when studying for courses in literature, the human-ities, mathematics, and science.

Reading Literary Works

When you are taking literature courses in college, you will be expected to read different genres, such as poems, novels, short stories, or dramas, not just for enjoyment, but also for study.

Reading Novels, Short Stories, and Drama   If you are reading nov-els, short stories, or drama, you cannot preview in the way described for textbooks, since literature is not written with neat headings and sub-headings. In addition, most people certainly do not want to know the end of a story or play before they read it!

However, if there is an introduction to the story or information about the author, as part of your preview, you should read these editorial aids carefully, noting important information. Many times your instructor will not tell you to read this information, but will expect you to do so.

In addition, if study questions are given at the end of the story, read all of them before you begin reading the assignment. It is a good idea to put a bookmark at the place where the questions appear. Because study questions in literary anthologies are usually sequential, keep the first question in mind as you begin to read. When you find the answer to that question, write in the margin a question similar to the question at the end of the story, and then highlight the key words that answer it. Also, as a cross-reference, write the page number(s) of where you found the answer next to the listed question at the end of the story. Read the second question and continue reading the story to find the answer, and so on. If your instructor gives you study questions, you should follow a similar process. Write your own questions in the margins and highlight key-word answers. Then write page numbers next to your study questions and jot down key words on that piece of paper.

In literature, the read-and-mark step will be used to identify important aspects of the work, such as ideas relating to the theme, traits of the major characters, significance of events, and so on. Depending on your reading assignment, you will have to adapt the read-and-mark method to meet the requirements of the instructor or the assignment. You most likely will have to discuss the assignment in class and write about characters, theme, and setting. Your marginal questions should include references to these major aspects of literature. Finally, you will need to know more than just the plot; you will need to interpret why events are happening and why characters do what they do. *Why* questions are very important.

As you are reading, you may have questions about what happened in the story or why a character makes a certain statement or acts in an unusual way. Jot these questions on another piece of paper (noting the page numbers) so that you won't confuse them with your read-and-mark questions. If you have questions, other students most likely will, too, and if you do not write your questions down, you may not remember what they are when you get to class.

Finally, each genre or type of literature has its own terminology and definitions. This means that you need to learn these terms and definitions so that you can recognize them as you read the assigned selections. If you are using an anthology in the course, it will generally have a glossary of literary terms at the end of the book, to which you can and should refer for the terms and their definitions.

Reading Poetry   Because the format in which a poem usually appears on a page differs from that of fiction or informative material, some people think it should be read line by line. On occasion, this method of reading might work, but rather than reading line by line, you should concentrate on reading a poem aloud, sentence by sentence, using the punctuation as a guide indicating when to pause or stop. In addition, poetry is usually much more condensed in meaning than prose, so you need to read a poem several times and think about the significance of every word.

As mentioned in the discussion on reading fiction and drama, be sure to read any explanatory information about the poet and the poem and any footnotes. Also, have a dictionary handy to look up unfamiliar words or references. Poets often use allusions, which are references to other works of literature, mythology, history, or the Bible. You may even need to go to the library to use a dictionary of mythology or a dictionary of the Bible to clarify some meanings if the text does not have footnotes explaining unfamiliar references.

Read the following untitled poem by Emily Dickinson, in which she praises the delight and benefits of reading. Look up any unfamiliar words in your dictionary.

> There is no frigate like a book
>   To take us lands away,
> Nor any coursers like a page
>   Of prancing poetry:
> This traverse may the poorest take
>   Without oppress of toll:
> How fragile is the chariot
>   That bears the human soul!

Anyone who tries to read Emily Dickinson's poem line by line may not be able to understand it. The poem, like most poems, is packed with images and verbal pictures. You need to read the poem aloud more than once, grouping the words and phrases according to punctuation, not according to lines, and replacing unfamiliar words with familiar ones. Sometimes, too, it is necessary to change the word order to clarify the meaning. Here is Emily Dickinson's poem transcribed into prose:

> There is no ship [frigate] that can take us to foreign places the way a book can (because we can go *anywhere* in time or space or distance by reading), nor any horse [courser] fast enough to match the pace and rhythm [prancing] of a poem.

> This (ability to read books and poems) is a road or a way to travel [traverse] that even people without money [the poorest] can take because they do not have to worry [without oppress] about paying a toll.

> How delicate [fragile] is the vehicle or body [chariot] that either holds, contains, or gives birth to [bears] a person's soul!

In the first six lines, Emily Dickinson is explaining the joys of reading prose and poetry, using several images of, and comparisons or contrasts to, traveling—frigate, courser, and paying tolls. The last two lines of the poem are the most complex because the verb *bear* has so many possible meanings and the meaning goes beyond the simple act of reading a book.

You might think of reading a poem as being similar to working a jigsaw puzzle: All the pieces are there; you just have to fit them together properly. Your marginal questions for the read-and-mark step will relate both to the meaning of the poem and to the poetic techniques that are used. Reading poems can be just as enjoyable as reading prose if you use your knowledge of *how* to read a poem to get meaning out of it.

Reading in the Humanities

STUDY-READ, as explained originally, works well in subjects like history, psychology, and sociology. However, instructors in these subjects often assign books, such as biographies, or articles to supplement or even to replace a text. These readings, most likely, will not follow the typical textbook format. In particular, they may not have introductions, headings, and summaries.

In approaching these nontext reading materials, first make sure you understand the instructor's reason for having you read them. For example, in a history course, you may be assigned a biography or novel just to get some background on the historical period you are studying. If that is

the case, you may not need to read in great detail because you just want to get the general idea. On the other hand, if you are going to be tested on the information, ask your instructor what kinds of information you need to know. The way you read and mark will be very different depending upon your goals. If you need to learn specific dates and names, you will have to take careful notes and write questions about as many facts and details as you can. If you just need to learn background information or get an overview of the topic, you will be looking for and writing questions relating to major ideas and trends. If the sources are library books or articles on reserve, you will need to do your read-and-mark step on summary paper.

Reading Mathematics

STUDY-READ should certainly be used for a math text, but some special considerations are in order for math reading. Math is much more than computation, the simple act of solving problems: Learning the concepts and principles behind the formulas and computations is equally important. There is a very big difference between just reading a formula and actually understanding what it means. You need to visualize the formula and verbalize the steps required to solve a problem. For example, if you have to find the distance traveled at a certain rate of speed, the formula is $d = rt$. However, knowing the formula is helpful only if you know what the formula means. In this case, the formula means "$d$istance is equal to $r$ate times $t$ime." So if a train travels at a rate of 90 miles per

hour for 6 hours, you need to multiply the rate (90 miles) by the time (6 hours), or $d = 90 \times 6$, which is 540 miles. The more complex formulas become, the more important it is that you focus on the *meaning* of the formula instead of just being able to repeat it.

Usually math teachers assign only one section of a chapter at a time. Because math courses are organized in a sequential way, with one concept leading to the next, it is very important that you understand each section before you go on to the next. In addition, you should always review the previous section or sections right before you preview the current assignment.

Your preview in math will be much more extensive than in other courses. In your preview, read the boldface print and new terms. But, in addition, quickly read the paragraphs of explanation the first time you actually read through the new section. Always read the introduction and summary during your preview. You may not understand everything, but be sure you read everything *before* you go to class.

In class, when the instructor works problems on the board, the explanations may seem crystal clear at the time, but when you get home that clarity may blur unless you have good notes. So take *lots* of notes. Good notes include not just the problems copied from the board but, more importantly, the explanations, the reasons, and the logic behind them. So write down as much as possible of the instructor's information.

You have read each section quickly during your preview; now you are ready to read and mark in depth. When you perform the second step in STUDY-READ, be prepared to read a section several times. Then, when you read and mark, concentrate on the explanatory information, asking yourself questions concerning definitions of terms and the main concepts, principles, or properties. This can be done in the text or on summary paper. Since you have already taken good class notes, you can refer to them as you read your text. Your goal is to understand the underlying concepts and principles and to follow the appropriate steps, not just to get the correct answer for an individual problem.

Most math chapters contain many problems for students to solve. Work all the problems assigned, using your marked text to help you understand the new concept. If you are to select the problems yourself, be sure to do a sampling of problems throughout the section and not just the first several problems. If you have time to do only a few problems, be sure to include application as well as computational problems. Really understanding a few well-selected problems is more valuable than mechanically working through many problems just to arrive at the correct answers given at the back of the textbook. Remember, your goal is to *understand* the *concepts*, not merely to get correct answers to specific problems. Try to reason through the examples so that you understand the elements in the problem. As you come across new terms, add them to your vocabulary.

Sometimes students who otherwise understand mathematical concepts are a bit puzzled by the reading of a word problem. When you are trying to solve a word problem, you need to be concerned with organizing the information in a way that allows you to form a plan for solving the problem. Although there is no one way to solve all word problems, the following four steps should help you read a problem and then work through it:

1. *Read.* Analyze the problem until you understand the situation and identify the question(s) you are being asked to answer.
2. *Organize.* Identify the knowns and unknowns. Using actual words, write out the relationships in the problem. Look up any unfamiliar mathematical terms or formulas needed to solve the problem. Make a chart, diagram, or picture if it will help you visualize your task.
3. *Model.* Form a mathematical model for the problem. When beginning word problems, this usually consists of translating the words into an algebraic statement such as an equation. To form the model, you must define mathematical vocabulary such as variables and expressions to represent words in the problem.
4. *Solve.* Find the solution to the mathematical model, and use it to answer the question in the word problem. Check the reasonableness of your answer, and state it in an English, not a mathematical, sentence.

The following example illustrates how to use these guidelines: A student's grades on three tests are 82, 94, and 75. What must the student score on the fourth test so that the average of the four tests comes out to 83?

First, you *read* the problem and learn that you are being asked to find the score on the fourth test. Second, you *organize* your facts. You already know the scores on the first three tests, and you know that you want the average of all four tests to be 83. You need to know how to find the average of four numbers. You may have to look in your textbook or notes to find the correct steps to take in order to make your model. Third, you can then form a *model* by defining a mathematical symbol, such as *x*, to represent the score on the fourth test. To find the average of four numbers, you add them up and divide by 4. You make a model of the needed relationship of "the average of the four tests is 83" with these mathematical symbols and numbers:

$$\frac{82 + 94 + 75 + x}{4} = 83$$

Finally, you need to use your knowledge of the subject of algebra to *solve* this equation. You find that $x = 81$. Since *x* represents the score on the fourth test, you can answer the question after checking that your result is reasonable. Your statement of the answer is, "The student must score 81 on the fourth test to get an average of 83 on all four tests."

Following these four steps will allow you to reach the solution for most word problems.

In the review-by-reciting step of STUDY-READ in math, you should review groups of similar problems you have worked and recite specifically *how* to do each step. To be sure you know how to work each formula, make up your own examples. It is imperative that you review both your notes and the chapter sections continually until you are certain that you understand the concepts and know the technical terms.

Reading in the Sciences

Reading science textbook assignments is very similar to reading math texts. Both require careful and detailed problem-solving skills and ana-

lytical reading. Previewing the text is especially important because it gives you background information, which allows you to read the text with an understanding of how each detail fits into the whole structure of the chapter. Pay particular attention to nonverbal materials. The diagrams, graphs, charts, and pictures found in all science texts illustrate details of processes, formulas, or reactions.

After the preview step, you are ready to read and mark, keeping in mind that you must account for all diagrams, as well as new terms and the information in the paragraphs. In order to read diagrams in science, you have to follow several steps. First, to get an overall idea of what the diagram is illustrating, read the general description in the text. An example of a scientific diagram, entitled "Figure 2.4" (Mader 20), is provided on the following page. In this diagram, the general description is found below the drawings: "Ionic Reactions: Gain/Lose Electrons." As you read the description, identify the special terms, which in this case are *ions* and *ionic reaction*. If these terms are not in your vocabulary at this time, you may need to take notes or create 3 x 5 cards.

After reading the general description, carefully read the information in the specific description, found in this illustration at the top of the page. Read this description step by step. As you are reading, follow the steps of the diagram, matching the written words with the visual picture. Try to visualize what is happening, making sure you understand how one step leads to or is related to the next. Continue with this procedure until you reach the last step of the process. Depending on the complexity of the material, you may have to repeat these steps until you clearly grasp the meaning of the diagram.

Finally, the best way to make sure you understand the concept depicted in the diagram is to make your own diagram. As you make your diagram, explain the process aloud. Use your diagram to study the process, always visualizing what is occurring as well as reciting the steps.

In science textbooks, as you read and mark, another focus will be to learn the terminology and formulas. It is essential that you look for new terms and definitions as you read and that you highlight them and use a system for keeping track of them (see Chapter 4).

When reading the actual information in the paragraphs, you should read and mark only one paragraph at a time, rather than a section, because each paragraph is packed with information. In fact, the information is so dense that you cannot depend on key words because most words are key words. Thus, if you mark the text too quickly, you will

Figure 2.4

Ionic reactions. **a.** When the neutral atom sodium (Na) becomes an ion, it loses an electron. It then has 8 electrons in the outer shell. The sodium ion (Na$^+$) has a positive charge because it has one more proton than it has electrons. **b.** When the neutral atom chlorine (Cl) becomes an ion, it receives an electron. It then has 8 electrons in the outer shell. The chloride ion (Cl$^-$) has a negative charge because it has one less proton than it has electrons. **c.** When sodium reacts with chlorine, sodium gives an electron to chlorine, and sodium chloride (Na$^+$Cl$^-$) results. The 2 ions are held together by their opposite charge in an ionic bond.

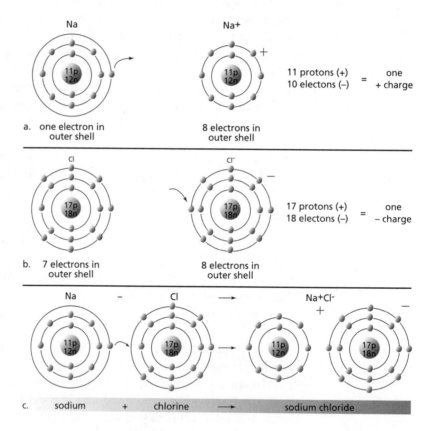

Ionic Reactions: Gain/Lose Electrons

In one type of reaction, atoms give up or take on electrons in order to achieve a completed outer shell. Such atoms, which thereafter carry a charge, are called **ions**, and the reaction is called an **ionic reaction**. In ionic reactions, atoms lose or gain electrons to produce a molecule that contains ions in a fixed ratio to one another. For example, figure 2.4 depicts a reaction between a sodium (Na) and chlorine (Cl), in which chlorine takes an electron from sodium. The resulting ions in sodium chloride (Na$^+$Cl$^-$) have 8 electrons each in the outer shell. Notice that when sodium gives up an electron, the second shell, with 8 electrons, becomes the outer shell.

tend to mark everything. To avoid overmarking the text, read each paragraph until you understand it. Try paraphrasing what has been said or, better yet, writing it in your own words. You will need to mark in the text *and* write information on a separate notebook page or the back side of your class notes. Because the sciences are so precise and the white space in the text is usually inadequate for all the information you need to learn, you should employ both methods simultaneously—highlighting pages in the text and writing questions and answers separately on paper. Be sure you put the textbook page numbers on the pages of your notes. The textbook marking can be used for *major* questions and highlighted answers. In addition, the separate notebook page or the back side of your class notes can be used to list other less major or more detailed questions and answers and your own illustrations.

The following paragraph from a biology book illustrates how packed full of information a science textbook can be:

CHLOROPLASTS: WHERE IT HAPPENS

The interior of a chloroplast contains stacks of membranous compartments called grana (sing. **granum**). The individual flattened sacs within each granum are called **thylakoids**. The green pigment **chlorophyll** is found within the membrane of the thylakoids, and it is here that solar energy is captured. Surrounding the grana is a fluid-filled space called the stroma. The **stroma** contains enzymes that participate in photosynthesis. (Mader 84)

As you read and mark this paragraph, you will realize how full of information it is. Your questions in the margin might be a pair of factual ones ("What is inside chloroplasts?" "What does each of these structures do?"), or you might choose to write a higher-level question ("Describe the structural arrangement of granum, thylakoids, chlorophyll, and stroma within a chloroplast."). With a paragraph like this one, you could easily fill the margin with questions and highlight almost every word! Thus, you would be wise to supplement text notations by using summary paper—either a separate notebook page or the back side of your class notes—so that you have room to write your questions and answers.

Additionally, your instructor will hold you accountable for all the terms. Whether you use 3 x 5 cards, the back side of your notes, or your own personal glossary of terms, you will have to learn these terms. For example, the "Chloroplasts" paragraph includes the following words that a student in the course should know how to define and spell: chloroplast, granum (pl. grana), thylakoids, chlorophyll, stroma, and photosynthesis.

In the read-and-mark step, in addition to writing questions and identifying technical terms, you should draw your own representation of the structure you are reading about—in this case, the inside of the chloroplasts. The drawing does not have to be anything fancy, nor do you have to be an artist: Just draw a picture (lines, stick figures, or whatever) of how you visualize the structure. Here is an example of what your drawing might look like:

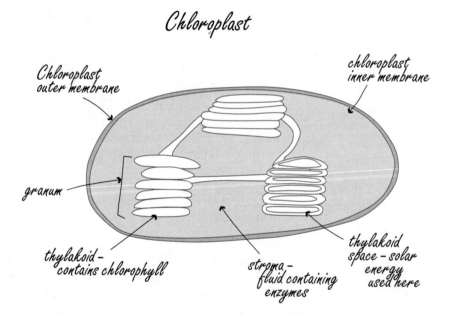

As you read any chapter in a science text, look for relationships such as cause and effect, comparisons and contrasts, processes, cyclic activity, patterns, or grouping. When you find such relationships, your questions in the margins or on summary paper might be phrased to show how structure relates to function, temperature to state of matter, or pressure to volume. Whenever you can, draw pictures showing these relationships and practice visualizing them in your mind. Your picture could even be a chart that would allow you to see similarities and differences or relationships in time or cause and effect (see Chapter 9 for examples).

In both the read-and-mark stage and the review-by-reciting stage, break the task into manageable segments. Do not try to overload your brain with too much material at one time. Also, because of the density of the information, you will want to review frequently by reciting manageable portions of the chapter until you have mastered the material. As in math, much of what you learn in the sciences is cumulative. You will be expected to understand the information so well that you can confidently apply it to the next process you are learning. You have to master one concept before you go on to the next, so review of previous material is a must.

Exercise 3-D

Directions: Go back to Chapter 1 and Chapter 2 and the beginning of this chapter and read and mark these pages. Then complete your mastery of STUDY-READ by reviewing the information by reciting.

Begin using STUDY-READ in all your classes.

Summary

In this chapter, you focused on the power of reading, specifically as it relates to reading college textbooks. Each quarter or semester, shortly after purchasing your textbooks, you should examine each whole textbook in order to familiarize yourself with the contents of each course and the layout of each textbook. After reading assignments are given in each class, you can master your textbook chapters by using the STUDY-READ method. This method of reading and studying a textbook involves three steps: preview, read and mark, and review by reciting. STUDY-READ is useful in all college textbook reading assignments, but some adaptations may be necessary in specific subjects, such as literature, the humanities, math, and science.

Chapter 4

The Power of Words

Not too long ago, one of the authors of this text went to the Seventh Annual Conference on Pedagogy. When she informed her students that Monday's class would be canceled because of this upcoming event, one student asked, "What is pedagogy?"

The teacher responded, "Pedagogy means the art or method of teaching."

The student replied, "Well, why didn't they just say that so everyone could understand it!"

"Actually," the instructor explained, "everyone who is going to the conference understands the word *pedagogy* because it is part of the technical vocabulary of teachers."

The preceding example serves as evidence that all courses and all disciplines have their own vocabulary. The sooner you learn the terms used in a particular course, the easier it will be for you to understand the material. Those of you, for example, who now own computers are aware of the "computer language" that is becoming more and more vital to a computer-literate society. Old words have taken on new meanings, and new words are being coined: Menus are not what you order from in a restaurant; an icon is not a religious image; windows are not what you look out of in a building. Bits, bytes, and baud rate; menus, icons, and windows; Mac, DOS, and Lotus; superhighways, Internet, and World Wide Web are just a small part of the computer language that every user needs to know.

The point is that computer technology, like other disciplines, has a language all its own. Therefore, to cruise smoothly down the highway of any new course, you need to plan a strategy for learning new vocabulary words and terms. Several different methods are available, and—depending on the course or discipline—you will have to determine which one or ones would be the most useful and appropriate.

In this chapter, you will review how to use a dictionary and how to benefit from its cousin the thesaurus. You will also learn three effective strategies for organizing and learning new vocabulary words and technical terms.

USING THE DICTIONARY

Dictionary use is certainly not new to you, but when you reach college, you may need to rediscover the value of the dictionary. The famous African American activist Malcolm X, while imprisoned, discovered the value of using a dictionary. He discovered that he needed to improve his reading and writing because these were then his major means of communication with the outside world. He says in *The Autobiography of Malcolm X,* "I became increasingly frustrated at not being able to ex-

press what I wanted to convey in letters that I wrote. . . . I saw that the best thing I could do was get hold of a dictionary—to study, to learn some words. . . . I'd never realized so many words existed!" (186–187). Malcolm X used the dictionary to improve his ability to read and write and to take himself far beyond his eighth-grade education to become a very articulate writer and sophisticated reader. You, too, can broaden your education by using a dictionary frequently.

Finding Definitions

In every course you take, you will encounter new terms. Perhaps in the past when you were reading, you simply skipped over words you did not know, hoping you could understand the material by guessing at the meaning, rather than stopping to look up the words in a dictionary. That is okay if you are just reading for fun and do not have the time or the curiosity to find out what the words mean. Guessing is also fine if the *context*—the surrounding words and sentences—reveals the meaning of a word to you, as often happens in textbooks. Then you can make an educated guess as to the word's meaning.

However, quick and unfounded guesses can get you into trouble in college courses. For example, one student in an English literature course wrote this sentence in her notes from a lecture: "Many empirical decisions were made in the mid-eighteenth century." Later, when she studied her notes, she thought, "Empirical, that must refer to the empire. George II was King of England then, so he must have made many decisions." The question in the margin of her notes became, "Why was Geo. 2 impt. in 1750s?" Since the sentence contained no context, she should have looked up *empirical* instead of randomly guessing at the meaning: It actually means "conclusions drawn from experiment or observation" and has nothing to do with royalty. You can guess what happened when she answered a question about that information on a test. The lesson to be learned from this incident is that you should *not* try to guess definitions of words in your courses when sentences, spoken or written, do not give you clear meanings.

Examining Dictionaries

You may have used a dictionary since grade school, but if it has been a long time since you *studied* how to use the dictionary, you may be overlooking some very valuable information that can be found in this useful tool.

As an adult enrolled in higher education, you should have a college dictionary, and, no, your old grade school one will not do. As you saw in the example of computer language, all language is changing and growing over time. A 1925 or even a 1975 dictionary will not be adequate today because the language is constantly changing. Look at the dictionary you currently use. Turn to the back of the title page to see when the dictionary was last revised. Is it time to go shopping?

When shopping for a new dictionary, you should examine several, if possible, to see what they contain before you buy one (see "Examining a Textbook" in Chapter 3). The three major college dictionaries—*Random House, Webster's New World,* and *The American Heritage*—are all good resources and come in both paperback and hardback editions. Hardback dictionaries contain much more information than paperback ones and, therefore, are preferable. However, each of the three hardback editions has different features besides the main feature, defining words.

In addition to definitions of each entry word, most dictionaries give synonyms and antonyms and a guide to correct usage. Besides these features, a hardback dictionary will have a variety of articles, appendixes, charts, pictures, tables of weights and measures, maps, or other unique features, such as a writer's manual of style. These features vary with each dictionary, so preview several editions and titles before you purchase one.

Understanding Dictionary Entries

Having examined your current dictionary, you are ready to consider the information that is available to you in a given entry. For purposes of study, the word *mnemonic,* which will be discussed in Chapter 8, will serve as a sample entry. In a dictionary, the entry will look something like this:

---

mne·mon·ic (nĭ-mŏn´ĭk) *adj.* Relating to, assisting, or designed to assist the memory. — **mnemonic** *n.* A device, such as a formula or rhyme, used as an aid in remembering. [Gk. *mnēmonikos,* from *mnēmōn, mnēmon-,* mindful.] — **mne·moń·i·cal·ly** *adv.* (*American Heritage College Dictionary*)

Every dictionary entry provides you with several different kinds of information. By looking at each part of the entry, you can discover what information is included. By analyzing the entry word *mnemonic,* you will gain an understanding of the major parts of a dictionary entry:

1. **mne·mon·ic** The entry word itself is divided into syllables as shown by dots. Of course, if it is a word, like **dog,** that has only one syllable, it will appear as one word with no separations. If the entry is really two separate words, like **shelf life,** no dot will appear.
2. (nĭ-mŏn´ĭk) The word in parenthesis represents the phonetic pronunciation; it is spelled the way it sounds, and marked with an accent (nĭ-mŏn´ĭk). The accent here is on the second syllable (mŏn´), which means that that is the syllable you stress when you say the word. You will find the key to the phonetic symbols at the bottom of the page in most dictionaries or at the beginning of the dictionary in some paperback editions. The key associates the phonetic symbols with simple words that everyone knows. This information allows you to pronounce the word correctly by matching the symbols and letters in the word to the pronunciation key in the dictionary. The pronunciation key from *The American Heritage College Dictionary* looks like this:

ă	pat	îr	**pier**	ŭ	cut
ā	pay	ŏ	pot	ûr	**urge**
âr	care	ō	toe	th	**thin**
ä	father	ô	paw	<u>th</u>	**this**

ĕ	pet	oi	boy	hw	**wh**ich
ē	be	ou	**out**	zh	vi**si**on
ĭ	pit	ŏŏ	took	ə	**a**bout, it**e**m
ī	p**ie**	ōō	boot	'	

Sometimes the entry includes alternative pronunciations and spellings. In addition, if the plural form of the word is made in some way other than by adding an *s,* the plural spelling is listed, too.

3. *adj.* and *n.* These abbreviations in the entry tell what part or parts of speech the word is. *Mnemonic,* for example, can be used as an adjective (*adj.*) or a noun (*n.*). The meaning of these abbreviations can be found in the front of the dictionary, usually in a section called "Guide to the Dictionary." For verb entries, the various forms of verbs are given, which is particularly helpful with irregular verbs such as *drink/drank/drunk.* For adjectives and adverbs, the dictionary provides not only the word (*big*) but the comparative form (big, *bigger*) and the superlative form (big, bigger, *biggest*).

4. "Relating to, assisting, or designed to assist the memory.— **mnemonic** *n.* A device, such as a formula or rhyme, used as an aid in remembering." The meaning of the word is the main part of the entry. Words may have only one meaning or several, a fact that is discussed later in this chapter.

5. [Gk. *mnēmonikos,* from *mnēmōn, mnēmon-,* mindful] The word origins (etymology), found in brackets, tell you where the word began and how other languages adopted it. In this case, *mnemonic* comes from Greek. Often the original root meaning is helpful in understanding the current word. Here the original root means "mindful."

6. **mne·mon′i·cal·ly** *adv.* At the end of the entry, you will find any other forms of the word that exist. In this case, mnemonic can be transformed into an adverb by adding "ly."

These six points are the major parts of all dictionary entries. Other possible types of information that are included in some entries, particularly in hardback dictionaries, include:

• Labels: The label tells you the area of knowledge to which the term applies (chem., bio., Eng., etc.); what usage is current (standard, slang, informal, archaic, etc.); what areas of the world use the word (Chiefly British, Australian, Irish); or what areas in the United States use the word (Southern U.S., Eastern U.S., Southwestern U.S., etc.).

- Cross-references: These notations tell you that additional information pertaining to this word (for example, synonyms and usage notes) is listed in another entry.
- Synonyms: Some entries will include a list of words with the same meaning as the entry.
- Usage notes: These special remarks provide you with information relating to diction, pronunciation, grammar, and acceptability of using certain words or phrases.

The following exercise will give you a chance to practice your dictionary skills and, possibly, introduce you to some new words.

Exercise 4-A

Directions: Look up the following words in your dictionary. Write down the phonetic spelling of the words, the part(s) of speech listed, and their meanings.

1. pneumatic _____

_____

_____

_____

_____

2. scintillate _____

_____

_____

_____

_____

3. xenophobia _____

_____

_____

_____

_____

By learning more about your dictionary and dictionaries in general, you will discover that dictionary entries, with their various features, are a rich and powerful source of information. Check the "Guide to the Dictionary" at the front of your dictionary to see which features are included.

Context Clues

As you are well aware, many words may have several meanings, often very different. Knowing this, in order to choose the correct definition, you must examine and understand a word in its context.

As an illustration, think about the familiar word *litter*. It has more than five separate meanings in a dictionary. Suppose, for instance, you came in on the tail end of a news announcement and the broadcaster said, "A famous scientist has been called in to examine the litter for clues."

Even if you know all the meanings of the word *litter*, without the *context* of the whole news report, you would be groping desperately for the exact meaning of the announcer's concluding words. Does the word *litter* refer to a device, like a stretcher, to carry a sick or injured person?

Is the announcer referring to the offspring of a cat or a dog? Or is he talking about the bedding material used for animals like horses and cattle? Could he be referring to the study of forestry and the examination of the uppermost layer of soil on the forest floor? Or, just maybe, is he referring to the trash or garbage that is dangerously polluting a certain river or stream?

The example above serves to illustrate the power of reading and listening intelligently through context. When you are uncertain of the meaning of a word, the words surrounding that new word will almost always help you understand the most appropriate meaning. However, when the context does not reveal the correct meaning, you need to reach for your dictionary.

Exercise 4-B

Directions: To heighten your awareness of the meanings of words, look up the following words and *list the number* of different meanings that are given:

1. frog _____

2. bear (as a verb) _____

Name the dictionary you used. _____

When you looked up the word *bear*, you should have noticed that there were two different entries. When one entry word has exactly the same spelling as another entry, the entries will be numbered to show that they are considered to be two separate and different words. When you are looking up an unfamiliar word, always check to see if more than one entry exists. If so, make sure you get the definition that makes sense in the context you are using.

Word Parts

A complete discussion of dictionaries needs to include word parts, since knowing word parts and their meanings can significantly increase your

Exercise 4-C

Directions: Look up the following words to see how many entries are listed. Then find the correct definition for the sentence in which the word is used.

# of Entries

_____ 1. **bat** The girl in the window *batted* her eyes at me.

Entry # _____ meaning: _____

_____ 2. **gill** I put my feet in the *gill*.

Entry # _____ meaning: _____

_____ 3. **butt** Please give me a *butt* of water.

Entry # _____ meaning: _____

_____ 4. **rap** I don't give a *rap* what he says.

Entry # _____ meaning: _____

vocabulary. This kind of information is especially valuable if you are taking science courses in which terminology is largely derived from Greek and Latin origins. Word parts includes prefixes, roots, and suffixes.

Prefixes are letters added to the beginning of a word that affect the meaning of that word. For example, knowing that the prefix *mono-* means "one," "single," or "alone" should help you understand many words that begin with *mono. Monosyllable,* for instance, means *mono-* + syllable, or one syllable. This same prefix is found in the words *monologue, monomania, monomial, monophobia, monoplane, monopoly,* and so on.

A *root* is a base word, the core or central part of a word that carries most of its meaning. For example, *spect* as a root means "to see," "to watch," or "to look at." It occurs, therefore, in such related words as *spectacles, spectator, inspect, respect, expectation, spectroscope, specter,* and so on.

Suffixes, the third kind of word parts, are letters added to the end of a word that usually indicate a part of speech or category to which it belongs. For example, building on the root word *gentle,* you can add different suffixes, thus changing the meaning slightly. Some words that would occur are *gentleman, gentlewoman, gently, gentleness, gentility, gentry, gentlest,* and even *gentleman's gentleman* (better known as a servant). Some suffixes are helpful because they give you a clear indication of the classification of a word. For example, *-hood, -ness,* and *-ship* all mean "state of," so we have words like *motherhood, friendliness,* and *relationship.* Likewise, *-ology* added to the end of almost any word indicates a branch of learning, such as *biology* or *psychology.*

The more prefixes, roots, and suffixes you become familiar with, the easier it will be for you to figure out unfamiliar words and to broaden your vocabulary.

Exercise 4-D

Directions: Look up the following prefixes, roots, and suffixes. Write the meanings of the word parts, and give several examples of words containing these parts that relate to the basic meaning.

Note: Words that are followed by a hyphen are prefixes, words without a hyphen are roots, and words preceded by a hyphen are suffixes.

1. *poly-* _____

_____

2. *anti-* _____

_____

3. *graph* _____

_____

4. *pseudo-* _____

_____

5. *hemo-* _____

_____

6. *script* _____

_____

(continued on the next page)

Exercise 4-D (continued)

7. *micro-* _____

_____

8. *photo* _____

_____

9. *-scope* _____

_____

10. *duc, duct* _____

_____

USING A THESAURUS

In addition to using a dictionary, you may also find it useful to consult a thesaurus (thĭ-sôr′əs). A *thesaurus,* according to *The American Heritage College Dictionary,* is "a book of synonyms, often including related and contrasting words and antonyms." In your writing or speaking, sometimes the right word may be just on the tip of your tongue, but you cannot think of it. The thesaurus is a good place to find *synonyms*—words having approximately the same meaning—or even *antonyms*—words with the opposite meaning.

If you are using a computer, a thesaurus is probably one of the features included in your word processing software. However, most computer thesauruses (also spelled thesauri) have a more limited selection of words than the book versions have.

The best-known thesaurus is *Roget's International Thesaurus.* Peter Mark Roget (rō-zhā′) began compiling a list of words in 1805 and published his first edition of the thesaurus in 1852. Then his son, John Lewis Roget, and later John's son, Samuel Romilly Roget, continued to revise and expand the book of words. Since then, others have continued to edit and revise it to keep the thesaurus up to date.

Synonyms in thesauri are usually arranged in one of two ways: (1) the index-to-word method or (2) alphabetical order.

In a thesaurus arranged by the index-to-word method, to find a synonym of the word, all you need to do is look up the word in the index to see where it is located. Although that sounds simple enough, it can start a complex series of actions on your part. For example, if you looked in the index of *Roget's International Thesaurus,* 4th ed., for the word *attend,* here is what you would find:

> **attend** accompany 73.7
> be a spectator 442.5
> be at 186.8
> ensue 117.3
> escort 73.8
> heed 530.6
> help 785.18
> listen 448.11
> result 154.5
> serve 750.13

Your first task is to determine which of the ten meanings of the word *attend* you wanted to find a synonym for because each one of these possible words will provide you with a whole list of synonyms. Suppose you wanted another word for "be at." In the index, "be at" refers you to the number 186.8. You would find the right page in the main section by using the guide numbers at the top of each page. Number 186.8 appears on the page between the guide numbers of 186.2 and 187.11. Here is what the entry 186.8 says:

> .8   **attend, be at,** be present at, find oneself at, go or **come to; appear,** turn up, show up [informal], show one's face, make or put in an appearance, give the pleasure of one's company, make a personal appearance, **visit, take in,** do [informal]; catch [informal]; sit in or at; be on hand, be on deck [informal]; watch, see; witness, look on, *assister* [Fr].

As you can see, you have many choices of alternative words. Boldface indicates that a word is also in the index; italics indicate that a word is foreign, in this case French. Now your task is to select just the right word or phrase that would be appropriate to substitute for "be at."

In a thesaurus arranged in alphabetical order, you simply look up a word alphabetically, just as you would when using a dictionary. In *Roget's II: The New Thesaurus* (3rd ed.), the entry word is followed by the part of speech, a definition, and then a list of synonyms. Each listing is complete in itself. Here is how the word *attend* appears in *Roget's II:*

> **attend** *verb*
> **1.** To occur as a consequence: ensue, follow, result. *See* CAUSE, PRE-CEDE. **2.** To be with or go with (another); accompany, companion,

company, escort. *Obsolete:* consort. **Idiom:** go hand in hand with. *See* AC-COMPANIED. **3.** To work and care for: do for, minister to, serve, wait on (or upon). *See* CARE FOR. **4.** To have the care and supervision of; care for, look after, mind, minister to, see to, tend, watch. **Idioms:** keep an eye on, look out for, take care (*or* charge) of, take under one's wing. *See* CARE FOR. **5.** To perceive by ear, usually attentively: hark, hear, heed, listen. *Archaic:* hearken. **Idiom:** give (*or* lend) one's ear. *See* SOUNDS.

Using a thesaurus can be very helpful. However, you must choose words from a thesaurus with some caution. Whenever you select a synonym, always make sure you know this new word well enough to understand what it implies. You don't want to sound pompous or be off the mark. Suppose you wanted a word to replace *happy* in this sentence: "He was very happy about getting a raise." If you blindly selected a word out of the list of synonyms, you might end up saying, "He was winsome about getting a raise." Although the word *winsome* is listed as a synonym for *happy*, it is inappropriate here because it means "charming, often in a childlike way," which is not what you wanted to say at all. A much better choice would be *overjoyed* or *elated:* "He was elated about getting a raise."

The thesaurus is a handy addition to any writer's personal library. However, be sure to use a thesaurus with care so that you choose only words that you are sure fit the meaning you want.

LEARNING TERMS AND VOCABULARY

Often, finding the definition of words is easy, but learning them can be a challenge. Most textbooks include the definitions of terms either within the text itself, in a glossary, or at the beginning or end of each chapter. In addition, you can identify many new terms in your textbook because they will be printed in italics, boldface type, or quotation marks. In lectures, teachers usually introduce new terms by giving definitions verbally, by writing them on the chalkboard, or by including them in class handouts. Learning new terms may seem like a simple task at the beginning of a course, but the number and complexity of the terms can soon mount up. Within a few weeks, you may begin to feel overwhelmed. Thus, early on, you will want to find an organized way to master the terms and vocabulary in each discipline.

As you discover new terms in your textbooks and notes, you should circle them, underline them, or highlight them (with a different color of highlight from the one you are using for notes) so that they clearly stand out. Then, to organize and study new terms in every discipline, you will want to adopt one or more of these three methods: Use 3 x 5 flash cards, list terms on the back side of your notes, or make your own personal glossary.

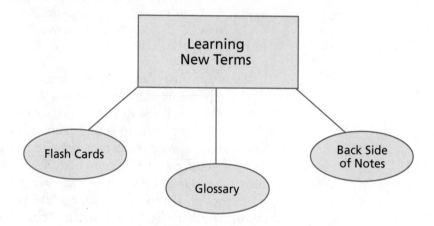

You may choose the method that best suits your learning style or needs. Or you may choose different methods for different courses or use a combination of methods, depending upon the subject matter and the number of technical terms.

Learning New Terms by Using Flash Cards

Creating 3 x 5 flash cards for vocabulary development is probably the best method in terms of flexibility because the cards are portable, and you can sort out what you know from what you do not know. You may have already used this method to learn your multiplication tables in math or to learn vocabulary words in a foreign language. To create your own set of cards, simply write the term on one side of the index card and the definition on the other:

Index Card

PEDAGOGY

text p. 22 or notes 5/17

the art or method of
teaching
or how a teacher teaches

side one   side two

Depending upon the course and the material you are studying, you may want to include other information on your cards. For example, you might want to include a cross-reference to the textbook page or your lecture notes (see the previous example). On the definition side of the card, you should write the formal definition and also your own definition because that will make it more meaningful to you. Side two could also be used to write examples or simple memory tricks or associations (discussed in Chapter 8). You might even draw a diagram or a picture that describes the term. These flash cards are your learning tools; include anything that will help you master the material.

Using flash cards is an excellent method of learning new words, especially in courses heavily weighted with technical terms. The cards are highly visual and tactile; that is, you can easily see the words and can handle and manipulate the cards. You can use them yourself or have someone help you study: a friend, a spouse, a child—anyone who can read. Furthermore, you can test yourself using either side of the card: Look at the word to recite the definition, or look at the definition to recite the term and spell it correctly. The ability to spell terms accurately can be very important. For example, in biology or anatomy and physiology, *ileum* means the third and lowest division of the small intestine, and *ilium* means the broad upper portion of the pelvis. Knowing when to use an *e* or an *i* could make the difference between passing and failing a test, or later, in a medical procedure, the difference between curing or killing a patient.

Finally, 3 x 5 cards are sturdy, extremely handy, and portable. Thus, if you carry some around with you, you can look at them whenever you have a few extra moments. Maybe you are a few minutes early for class—pull out your note cards. Maybe you are standing in a long line to get tickets for a Jimmy Buffett concert—pull out your note cards. Maybe you're sitting in the waiting room of a doctor's or dentist's office—pull out your note cards. Develop the habit of carrying cards with you at all times.

When you believe you know a term, set the card aside for a while. Later on, get out the "learned" cards and test yourself to see if you really do know those terms. After a period of time, try them at least once more. If you still know them well, you can safely assume that the terms are stored in your long-term memory.

Learning New Terms by Using the Back Side of Notes

You may want to keep your new vocabulary words with your notes. If you take notes on one side of the page, then you can use the back side of the page for your new terms. If your terms and definitions are added next to and parallel with the relevant notes, you will be able to study your terms more easily. See the following example:

Back Side for Terms   **Front Side for Notes and Questions**

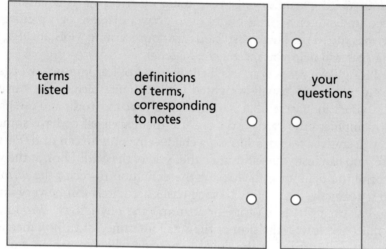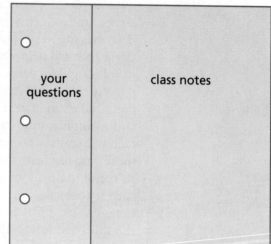

| terms listed | definitions of terms, corresponding to notes | | your questions | class notes |

Summary Paper

You can enter terms on the back side of your notes during class as you hear the words or after class when you Edit or Ask questions in your notes. Write the word in the three-inch margin and the definition in the five-inch space of your summary paper. Thus, you can cover one side or the other to recite your terms and definitions out loud. Simply looking over the list or rereading the words is not an effective way to learn the terms. You can easily study the terms by covering up either the term itself or the definition and reciting the answer.

Learning New Terms by Making Your Own Glossary

Just as textbooks often have a glossary of terms at the end of each chapter or at the end of the book, you might want to keep your own glossary for each course. Determine where you want to keep it in your notebook—at the beginning of your notes for each class or at the end. The words, of course, will be listed in the order in which they occur in your lectures or by chapters in the textbook. The format will be just like that of your terms on the back side of your notes, but now you will have them all together. Like flash cards, you can take this personal, self-made glossary out of your binder and carry it anywhere, which enables you to study at any time and at any place.

Summary

An awareness of new words and a solid knowledge of dictionary use are great aids in increasing your vocabulary and mastering technical terms. Owning an up-to-date college dictionary is important. Hardback editions are more useful than paperbacks. Each word entry in a dictionary provides you with a great deal of information concerning pronunciation, parts of speech, and various meanings. In addition, when you meet new words that have various meanings, context clues can help you figure out the best, most logical meaning. Learning word parts—prefixes, roots, and suffixes—will also make learning new words easier. Knowing the kinds of information your dictionary contains can unlock a world of knowledge for you.

Using a thesaurus to find synonyms can help you in your writing if you use this resource wisely. Since words have various shades of meaning, you should be very selective about choosing a synonym.

Finally, this chapter describes three systems of organizing and studying new terms. Using a systematic way to learn vocabulary words and technical terms in all your courses is essential because every discipline has its own language. The three recommended methods of mastering vocabulary are creating 3 x 5 flash cards, using the back side of your notes, and preparing a glossary, or you might adopt a combination of these systems.

Exercise 4-E

Directions: Now that you know three methods for learning terms, you need to use one or more of those methods to master the terms in this textbook. Also, incorporate a system for learning terms into all of your other courses.

Chapter 5

The Power of Self-Knowledge

Who knows you better than yourself? After all, you have been inside your skin for *x* number of years. Until you actually begin to explore what makes you tick, however, you may not know yourself as well as you think you do; you may not be making the most of yourself and your talents.

The focus of this chapter is you yourself and your personal preferences. Would you rather get up early or stay up late? Do you learn better by listening to a teacher or by reading a textbook? Are you more comfortable working alone or with others? Your answers to these questions and others indicate your preferences.

To get the most out of this chapter, it is important that you understand the differences between preferences and nonpreferences. *Preferences* refer to those actions and attitudes that feel natural, comfortable, easy, and stress-free, requiring little energy. *Nonpreferences* imply the opposite. These actions and attitudes may feel uncomfortable, awkward, and stressful, requiring extra effort.

This chapter will examine certain key factors concerning you and your preferences as a student and will demonstrate how an awareness of these factors can add to your self-power. In particular, you need to be in tune with your body's clock, your preferred learning style, your level of motivation, and your personality type. You need to have more self-knowledge and apply that knowledge to make you a more effective student.

PEAK TIMES

Everyone's body has its own internal clock. That is why some people say, "I'm a night person," while others say, "I'm a morning person." These times are considered *peak times,* meaning the times when you are best able to perform physical and mental activities.

You probably already know when you are most alert, but you may need to explore your own time clock in more detail.

Exercise 5-A

Directions: Answer the following questions in order to determine your peak time:

1. If you did not set your alarm, what time would you get up in the morning? _____

2. If you did not have any responsibilities tomorrow, how late would you stay up tonight? _____

3. If you have the chance, would you take a nap? Yes? _____ No? _____ What time of day? _____

4. What time of day do you prefer doing something mentally stimulating, like reading a book, writing a letter, balancing your checkbook, or making a decision? _____

5. What time of day do you prefer doing a physical task or activity, such as exercising, cleaning the house, washing the car, walking, swimming, or doing yard work? _____

If you answered the first question by giving a time before 9 A.M., indicating you get up early even without an alarm clock, you probably are a morning person. If possible, you should schedule classes early in the day or set aside morning hours to study. If you are not a night person but are forced to study late at night, you will not get as much accomplished as you would have if you had studied during your peak time. Early birds should also avoid enrolling in a night class.

In response to the second question, if you generally go to bed at 11 P.M. or later and enjoy staying up into the wee hours of the morning, you are a night person. You might have so much energy at 2 o'clock in the morning that you find yourself buzzing around the house doing a load of wash, cleaning your room, or fixing a pizza. Although in most colleges you cannot take a class at 2 A.M., you can harness this nighttime energy to write a paper, review your notes, or study your vocabulary or terms. It would also make sense for late sleepers to avoid scheduling an 8 A.M. class.

If your response to the third question, about taking naps, was no, then you can skip the rest of this paragraph. If, on the other hand, you answered yes, you need to keep reading. You may find yourself feeling drowsy or dozing off at a time when you are at your physical and mental low point, the opposite of your peak time. If possible, do not schedule classes at that time or try to study difficult subjects because that would be counterproductive.

Your responses to questions four and five, indicating when you prefer to be mentally and physically active, should give you clear evidence of your peak time. Some circumstances can interfere with using your peak time to its best advantage. However, even if you cannot use your peak time to study or take a class, you can at least understand why you are more alert and productive at certain times and less so at other times. Recognizing your peak time is just the beginning of self-knowledge.

LEARNING STYLES

Everything you learn comes through your five senses. From the time you are born, you use your five senses to learn about yourself and the world around you. For example, small babies spend hours looking at their hands and feet: sense of sight. Those same babies are soothed to sleep by lullabies: sense of sound. From firsthand experience, they learn that stoves are hot and ice cubes are cold: sense of touch. As they grow older, they put everything from rocks to cat food in their mouths: sense of taste. Finally, they are suddenly drawn to the kitchen when chocolate chip cookies are baking: sense of smell. A child, like all learners, uses all five of his or her senses to become acquainted with the world.

As an adult, you still rely on your senses to acquire information, even though your learning at this point is more sophisticated than that of a small child. Granted, you seldom learn in college by tasting your textbooks, or smelling them, for that matter, but your other three senses are still hard at work.

Learning occurs when you take in information by sight, sound, or touch. Thus, you may be primarily a visual learner, an auditory learner, or a tactile (also called kinesthetic) learner. *Visual* learners prefer to *see* information, *auditory* learners prefer to *listen to* information, and *tactile* learners prefer *hands-on* experience. Although you can learn by using any one, two, or all of these senses, you probably have a *preferred* learning style. No one sensory preference is better than any other, but an awareness of your preference is another way to help you get the most out of your study sessions and classes.

Exercise 5-B

Directions: In order to determine your preferred learning style, read each descriptive sentence. If you say, "Yes, that is usually true of me," put a check next to that sentence. Leave the line blank next to those sentences that do not apply to your learning style. Check as many or as few sentences in each category as apply to you.

Gaining meaning from seeing

_____ I prefer having written directions.

_____ Don't tell me, show me.

_____ I have to see a word written out to tell if it is spelled correctly.

_____ I like to use maps, pictures, and charts.

_____ I usually remember where I saw an item in printed material.

_____ I prefer to read things for or by myself.

_____ I take lots of notes in class and write "to-do" lists.

_____ I read labels on cans, signs, notices—anything that's available.

_____ I notice differences in colors, shapes, and forms.

_____ I need to write out math problems, see them written, or use flash cards.

Gaining meaning from listening

_____ I prefer to have oral directions.

_____ Don't show me; tell me.

_____ I need to sound out words (using phonetics) in order to pronounce them.

_____ I like to work in study groups.

(continued on the next page)

Exercise 5-B (continued)

Gaining meaning from listening

_____ I would rather listen to oral reports than read written ones.

_____ I like to interview people or get information from talking to them.

_____ I enjoy the sounds of words and like to play word games.

_____ I'm good at remembering jokes or the words to songs, jingles, rhymes, and limericks.

_____ I think it is fairly easy to learn foreign languages.

_____ I learn math best by having someone explain it orally.

Gaining meaning from hands-on activities

_____ I prefer doing or experimenting with things like computers, rather than reading directions or manuals.

_____ I like to manipulate objects physically.

_____ I learn to spell words by writing them out.

_____ I enjoy handicrafts—cross-stitching, sculpting, building models, etc.

_____ I am mechanically inclined.

_____ I find texture to be important in decorating or selecting clothing.

_____ I like to "talk with my hands."

_____ I enjoy being physically active (I don't like to sit still!).

_____ If I am learning something, I need to "walk through" the steps.

_____ I like to learn by using contour maps, scientific models, or other touchable materials.

Count up how many check marks you have in each of the three sections. The section in which you have the highest number of checks indicates your preferred learning style. You may have the same number (or almost the same) in two categories. That simply means that you are equally comfortable processing information with either of those senses.

If you had an equal number of answers in every section, you are quite adaptable. Most people, however, prefer one or two learning styles.

The number of sentences each person checks will also vary. Studies indicate that the older you are, the more likely you are to check more statements in every section. Obviously, adults returning to college have had more life experiences, which may enhance their learning and increase their adaptability.

Once you know your preferred learning style or styles, you can assess the best ways to enhance your classroom activities and your studying.

Visual Learners

Visual learners find reading assignments more to their liking than auditory or tactile learners do. In fact, almost all educational material is geared to visual learners. Thus, in class, if you are a visual learner, you will benefit most from viewing films, slides, transparencies, and information written on the board. Your learning is enhanced by reading handouts, charts, graphs, maps, and sample assignments or papers and by viewing molecular models or skeletons. You will also benefit from using a second textbook on the subject and comparing the information in the two books. Doing computer exercises or writing with a word processor will provide you with additional visual reinforcement. Typically, a visual learner who uses a computer likes to make a printed copy of the material in order to mark it for revisions. Because lecture notes provide you with visual reinforcement, you need to take plenty of notes so that you will have a good visual record of the lecture. Any visual organizers that you devise yourself—topic grids, action–reaction arrows, Ts, webs, and time lines—will help you remember the information (see Chapter 9).

Auditory Learners

Because auditory learners process information by listening, they are naturally more comfortable in lecture classes than visual or tactile learners might be. Auditory learners have an advantage because many college classes are primarily lectures. As an auditory learner taking notes in the classroom, you will benefit considerably from the T step of GREAT: testing yourself by reciting. Reciting *aloud* should be an easier, more natural learning skill for you than for visual or tactile learners.

When you read a textbook assignment, you might also consider reading aloud. The use of a tape recorder—not necessarily in the classroom, but as a study aid—will also enhance the learning of an auditory person. For example, you could record questions on the tape recorder, then pause, leaving blank space to recite the answers. When you are ready for your own recitation, you simply play the taped questions and fill in the blank segments with your verbal answers. If you are taking a foreign language, you could tape conversations or vocabulary, again with blank time for responses. You could play these tapes in the car while you are driving to and from school or work. With a little bit of thought, you might devise some other ways to use a tape recorder.

Finally, as an auditory learner, you may want to join study groups for some subjects. Study groups directly support the auditory learner's preference and, at the same time, allow the learner to gain different perspectives from fellow group members.

Tactile Learners

Tactile learners, who learn best through the sense of touch, generally prefer courses that have lab components, such as biology, chemistry, dental hygiene, or nursing. However, most learning situations cater to visual or auditory learners, so tactile learners must devise ways to use their hands-on talent for learning. As a tactile learner, you want to enhance your learning by adding a physical component when possible. For example, using the computer gives you a hands-on approach to learning. You might consider working with models or prototypes whenever possible. When some tactile learners STUDY-READ, they not only highlight or underline their text, but also write questions and key-word answers on summary paper. Many tactile learners endorse frequent use of 3 x 5 flash cards for vocabulary, terms, math and science formulas, and other learning concepts. In addition, although you should have a regular place to study, you might benefit from walking around as you recite. Tactile learners seem to absorb more information if they move about.

Complementing Your Preferred Learning Style

Knowing your preferred learning style will provide you with a powerful way to get the most out of your learning. However, you should also try to develop more strength in your less preferred styles. Since all knowledge is gained through the senses, the more senses you engage in your learning, the more likely you are to remember the information. Also, practice in nonpreferred styles gives you versatility in learning. Always keep an open mind and be willing to try new approaches.

Teachers' Styles and Classroom Settings

Instructors teach in different ways because they are influenced in part by their own preferred learning styles. Think about all the teachers that you have had in the past and that you have this term. They all have unique teaching styles and techniques. Whether you consider their teaching styles "good" or "bad" depends to some degree on what learning style you prefer. If your style matches that of the teacher, then that match may facilitate your success in that class. For example, if you are an auditory learner, you will have an advantage over visual or tactile learners in a class where an instructor teaches only through lectures. If, however, your style is a mismatch with that of your teacher, then you need to recognize the difference and work a bit harder in the class to adjust to that teacher's style. Mismatches cannot be used as an excuse for not learning. Such differences can be opportunities to develop a nonpreferred style.

Besides being knowledgeable about instructors' teaching styles, you also may want to consider the various classroom settings, which are most often determined by the teacher. Basically, classroom settings can be described as teacher-centered, student-centered, or project-centered.

Teacher-centered classes are primarily conducted through the traditional lecture method. Typically, the teacher stands in the front of the room lecturing, and students sit at desks in rows, listening and taking notes.

In the *student-centered* classroom, classes are often conducted through small- or large-group discussions, peer readings, and student presentations or debates. In this setting, students, teachers, and furniture tend to be organized in a way that suits the activity planned for a particular day. Teachers who use the student-centered setting are often more experimental and flexible in their approaches.

Project-centered settings are almost always labs. In these settings, students have specific projects or tasks to complete by themselves or with partners. Examples of project-centered settings include computer labs, science labs, writing labs, language labs, nursing labs, dental hygiene labs, and business labs.

As you may have observed, several combinations of these three settings can exist in some classrooms. For example, particularly in a three-hour class, a teacher might give a mini-lecture, then divide the class into groups for discussion, and then have students go to a lab to complete a hands-on project.

If you have a choice of teachers for a given course, you can consult other students who have taken the course and schedule the class according to which setting you prefer. For other courses, you will not have a choice, and you will need to adapt to a nonpreferred classroom setting.

MOTIVATION

Another aspect of knowing yourself is understanding what motivates you. As a human being, you are very complex and generally have a variety of motivations. For example, although you may eat because you are hungry, a primary motivator, you also eat because someone says, "Time for supper," or you look at your watch and say, "I've got an hour before my next class; guess I'll go get something to eat." Sometimes you may eat to relieve stress, anger, or boredom, or just to please your taste buds. The possibilities for what might motivate you can be quite varied.

When you were a child or a teenager, motivation was probably less complicated. You did what you wanted to do, or very often you did what you were told to do by a parent or another adult in charge. Do any of the following statements sound familiar, or, if you are now a parent, do you hear yourself saying words like these?

"It's time to put away your toys."

"I will read just one more story, and then you have to go to bed."

"You have to do your homework before you go out."

"Clean your room first; then you can go to a movie."

When you were a child and even a teenager, your choices and actions were often dictated by others who were responsible for you. In one sense, that is good because children do need guidance. However, now that you are a college student, you need to become responsible for yourself and your own decisions. In other words, you should strive to be a self-motivated person. Examining what motivates you can help you understand your actions better, which allows you to gain more control.

Exercise 5-C will give you an opportunity to begin thinking about your motivation.

Exercise 5-C

Directions: Answer each question by checking the appropriate line.

	Yes	Partly	No
1. I am going to college to get a degree.	____	____	____
2. I am in college because my friends are.	____	____	____
3. I study because I know I should.	____	____	____
4. I regularly procrastinate when I should be studying.	____	____	____
5. I don't think instructors grade me fairly.	____	____	____
6. I am responsible for the grades I receive.	____	____	____
7. It is not my fault if I don't attend class.	____	____	____
8. I don't finish my assignments on time because I'm a busy person.	____	____	____
9. I tend to be an unlucky person.	____	____	____
10. My grades directly relate to how thoroughly I study.	____	____	____

If you answered "yes" to 1, 3, 6, and 10 and "no" or "partly" to the rest of the questions, you are likely to be a self-motivated person. If most of your responses to 2, 4, 5, 7, 8, and 9 were "yes," then you may be letting the outside world control you too much.

Motivation and Locus of Control

A psychologist named Julian B. Rotter introduced the term *locus of control* in 1966. Locus means "place." If you place responsibility for your life within *yourself,* then you are said to have *internal locus of control.* On the other hand, if you place primary responsibility for your life on others and on circumstances outside yourself, then you are considered to have *external locus of control.*

People who are self-motivated have developed internal locus of control and are generally positive thinkers who are responsible for their actions. For example, if they cannot get to school, they do not blame their car for breaking down or a child for being sick. They have alternative plans already in place—a ride from someone else, a baby sitter, or a classmate who takes good notes and agrees to share them in an emergency. If they do not do well on a test, they say, "What did *I* do wrong?" and then analyze how they can improve their study habits in order to do better.

People who need to be pushed by other people or circumstances have external locus of control and are often very negative, blaming the world around them or "fate" when things don't go their way. They can be heard making comments like these:

"It's not *my* fault the car wouldn't start!"

"I wasn't able to do the work because my baby kept me up all night."

"I don't think the teacher went over half the stuff on that test. No wonder I didn't do well."

"How can I be expected to study when I have to work all night?"

Besides blaming cars, jobs, or others, people who have external locus of control may turn to drugs or alcohol to "solve" their problems instead of attacking the problems themselves. This so-called solution could lead to their being even less in control of their lives.

Obviously, dealing with serious situations that are not under your control is difficult. However, you do have the power to determine your actions and reactions. For example, even though you cannot control a health problem or a family crisis, you can determine how to accept the situation, face the reality of it, adjust your plans and goals, and move on with as positive an attitude as possible.

The following chart indicates some of the major differences between the attitudes of people with internal locus of control and people with external locus of control:

Locus of Control

=

where you place responsibility for control over your life

– External	+ Internal
Other people or things seem to control me.	I'm responsible for myself.
Others must push me.	I make my own choices.
My outlook on life is often negative.	My outlook on life is usually positive.
Professor Smith *gave* me a D!	I worked *hard* for this C!
I don't like change. I have my *own* ways of doing things.	Changing wasn't easy, but now I'm glad I did.
I'm unlucky. I never get any breaks!	Sure, I've had some bad breaks, but they're not an excuse to quit.
It's not my fault! I couldn't help it.	I take full responsibility for what happened.
I give up! I can't do anything about it.	I made a mistake. Now I'll figure out how to correct it.

External locus of control actually takes away your own self-power when you point the finger of blame at other people or at your surroundings or circumstances.

In order to achieve internal locus of control and self-motivation, you have to be willing to give up the security of making excuses and to take responsibility for *all* your decisions and actions. A person with internal locus of control has successfully made the transition from childhood to adulthood. With an awareness of locus of control, you can replace the tired, external cliché of "It's just not fair!" with the internally motivated challenge of "So, life is not fair; now, how can I solve the problem?" The decision and the placement of control and motivation are yours for the taking.

Exercise 5-D

Directions: Here are statements that a person with external locus of control might make. Explain what a person with internal locus of control might do to motivate him- or herself. Be prepared to share your answers in class.

1. "I signed up for a class; that teacher can't expect me to go to labs, too!" _____

_____

_____

2. "I don't know why I have to take this class." _____

_____

_____

3. "This instructor is so boring I can hardly stay awake." _____

_____

_____

4. "Why do I get all the tough teachers and you get all the easy ones?" _____

_____

_____

Positive Self-Talk and Visualization as Motivators

Have you ever said to yourself, "I *know* I'm going to fail (this quiz, this test, this final, this course)"? If you tell yourself often enough that you cannot do something, your *self* will believe it, and you will probably become incapable of achieving your goals. Psychologists call this phenomenon a *self-fulfilling prophesy*—you predict what you are going to do, and then you psychologically work for or against yourself to make it happen. If your prediction about yourself is negative, full of doom and gloom, then you are likely to have a negative outcome.

Fortunately, however, a self-fulfilling prophesy can go in the opposite direction as well. If you see yourself as successful and reinforce this vision with positive words, then you'll have a better than average chance of successfully achieving your goals. This *positive self-talk*, telling yourself that you can achieve your goals, should greatly increase your chances of success. In other words, your mind is willing to accept the "truth" as you see it; your mind knows only what you tell it. Why not fill your mind with good, positive, successful words and images as a means of achieving your goals?

The opposite of positive self-talk is *negative self-talk*, and it is guaranteed to drag you down. Have you ever met anyone who is constantly negative? That person makes a habit of belittling ideas and opportunities, often even before they have been explored or discussed. Such people make all

---

Exercise 5-E

Directions: Turn these negative self-talk statements into positive self-talk. Be prepared to share your statements in class.

1. "I'll never get this assignment finished!" _____

   _____

2. "I hate math!" _____

   _____

3. "I can't learn this material!" _____

   _____

kinds of negative statements, such as, "That won't work." "You shouldn't even try to do it that way." "Boy, that will be disastrous." "I couldn't do that if I tried, so I won't." This kind of talk and attitude is self-defeating and can result in inaction and hopelessness. Sure, at times you will feel "down"; that is only normal. Everyone has bad days. However, you should try to replace negative self-talk with positive self-talk and, if you can, remove yourself from others who have made negativity a habit or even a way of life.

Another form of positive self-talk is called mental visualization. *Mental visualization* involves actually picturing yourself as successful. People in all walks of life use this technique to build their confidence. Golfers, for example, visualize what they must include for the perfect stance, grip, swing, and follow-through to make the perfect tee shot or the perfect putt. Public speakers envision their ideal audience, eager and receptive, hanging on their every word and applauding wildly at the conclusion of the speech.

In the same way, when faced with a difficult task, you can envision yourself performing at your best. For example, you visualize yourself taking a test in your hardest subject. You see yourself entering the room, sitting in your usual seat, getting the test, beginning to calmly answer the questions, completing the test successfully, and handing it in to the instructor. You may even want to extend this vision to when you get the test back with a very good grade on it. Having visualized success, you will feel more confident when the actual experience happens.

Adopting a positive mental attitude and using positive self-talk and visualization will definitely increase your chances for success. Like the little engine struggling up the mountain in the children's story who said, "I think I can; I think I can; I *think* I can®"—and he could—you, too, can use mind over matter in the successful achievement of your goals.

PERSONALITY PREFERENCES

Not only is your learning affected by the use of your senses, it is also affected by your personality type. Your personality type influences such areas of learning as (1) your source of energy, (2) your methods of taking in information, (3) your means of making decisions, and (4) your approaches to work and play. These four categories may be discussed in terms of four pairs of opposites:

1. Extraverts or Introverts (sources of energy)
2. Sensors or iNtuitives (methods of taking in information)

3. Thinkers or Feelers (means of making decisions)
4. Judgers or Perceivers (approaches to work and play)

Each of these terms refers to personality preferences and is based upon the research of Carl Jung and Katharine Briggs and Isabel Briggs Myers. (*Note*: The word *Extravert* is purposely spelled with an *a* to conform to the official spelling on the personality preference survey.)

In 1923, some of the writings of Carl Jung, a Swiss psychologist, were published in English. He proposed the Theory of Motivation and Personality which describes people as being predominantly Extraverts or Introverts, Sensors or iNtuitives, and Feelers or Thinkers. The meanings and implications of these paired, opposite terms will be explained throughout the rest of this chapter.

Katharine Briggs, who had long been interested in differences among people's personalities, had previously and independently made similar observations about her friends and acquaintances in terms of their life-styles and personality preferences. When Jung's findings were published in the United States, she read his works and recognized the similarities to her own studies, and then she and her daughter, Isabel Briggs Myers, continued their research. Subsequently, they began developing a systematic and reliable way to understand differences in people. Their inventory, which was first published for public use in the 1970s, is called the Myers-Briggs Type Indicator (MBTI). This mother-daughter research team added an additional paired category to the personality preferences recognized by Jung, namely, Judgers and Perceivers.

If you want to take the official MBTI survey, a trained, qualified individual who can interpret the data and explain the results accurately must administer it. Many colleges and universities have a qualified MBTI person on the staff who will administer the inventory free or at a minimal cost. Taking the official MBTI survey and having it interpreted by a qualified person is really the only reliable way of knowing your true preferences. However, if such a resource is unavailable to you, you can get a sense of your personality preferences by reading the following explanations of the four pairs of contrasting preferences mentioned above.

As you read about the categories of the MBTI, it is essential to remember that all preferences are *good*. When you are able to operate according to your preferences, you feel comfortable and normal. However, since this is not a perfect world, you will sometimes have to work outside your preferences. This may make you feel awkward and uncomfortable, but you still have the ability to function in these situations.

Once you use your preferences for a period of time, they tend to become habits. A simple comparison might be found in such an everyday occurrence as putting on your shoes and socks. Do you start with the left foot or the right? It really doesn't make any difference which foot you start with, but you probably always begin with the *same* foot. The way you perform this action demonstrates your preference. Now try putting your socks and shoes on in the opposite way. How did that feel? You may not have been as comfortable because you were using your nonpreference.

Like the right and left foot illustration, the preferences in the four categories of the MBTI are set up as opposites. As you consider these categories, you will probably identify more with one preference than with the other. Your *honest* responses are important here. You will recognize yourself in parts of both opposites; however, you will usually feel more identification with one than with the other because that one is your preference.

No matter what your preferences are, view them as an empowerment or strength for you, not as an excuse for dodging responsibilities.

Extraverts and Introverts

The first pair of opposites deals with where you get your energy and how you interact with others. *Extraverts* (E) get energy from people and the outside world, whereas *Introverts* (I) find their energy from within themselves. Read the following descriptions to see which of the two opposites applies to your personality.

You are an Extravert (E), as the name implies, if you are energized by being with people and talking to them. In fact, you usually prefer talking rather than listening to others, and you may even speak before you have given a topic much thought. At times you say to yourself, "I wish I'd kept my mouth shut!" Right or wrong, you often respond quickly to questions in class. Additionally, you like to talk about writing assignments before you begin putting words on paper. You enjoy working in groups and sharing ideas, not only with friends but also with strangers. The lure of the outside world may distract you from studying, and you may procrastinate about spending time alone to study. Socially, you know a great number of people and consider many of them good friends. You enjoy parties and talking on the phone. Most activities involving people give you added energy.

If you are an Introvert (I), you are energized by being alone or with a small group of close friends. In class, you usually ponder your answer so carefully before you say anything that by the time you are ready to respond to a question, an Extravert may have already answered it. When you get a writing assignment, you would rather think about it before you start writing. You prefer working alone and sometimes resent other people taking up your time or calling on the phone. You can get so wrapped up in your own projects that you sometimes forget the deadlines set by the outside world. Socially, you may be considered quiet and shy. You generally have two or three very close friends and may hesitate to attend large social events, although you may enjoy yourself once you are there. After you have participated in a large group activity, you often feel drained of energy and need time alone in peace and quiet to recuperate.

Having read the descriptions of an Extravert and an Introvert, you may now be able to determine which term best describes you. Of course, you may very well have characteristics of both an E and an I, but one most likely is your preference. Check *one* of the following:

I am primarily an E _____, or I am primarily an I _____.

Sensors and iNtuitives

The next two categories, Sensors (S) and iNtuitives (N), indicate the way you prefer to learn information. (The abbreviation for iNtuitives is the letter N because the letter I has already been used as an abbreviation for Introverts.)

If you are primarily a *Sensor*, you depend heavily on your five senses to learn. You are considered practical and down-to-earth. You like to have information given to you in a clear, step-by-step way. For example, if you are given an assignment, you want specific directions about the content, format, length, and due date. In your writing, you are very good at including details, but you may have difficulty tying all these details together. In other words, as the old saying goes, "You often can't see the forest (the big picture) for the trees (the details)." During lectures, you prefer to have information presented sequentially, and you are more comfortable with facts than with theories or generalizations. You are tuned in to the present and do not worry much about the past or the future. Reality is more important to you than fantasy or imagination. You tend to read magazines and books from front to back and wonder why some people would open a magazine in the middle or read the last pages of a book first. At work, your focus is more on your own job than on its relationship to the whole project or company. Generally, you take the attitude of, "If it ain't broke, don't fix it." You don't understand why some people always want to change things; you are happy with the way things are.

If you are an *iNtuitive* person, your preferred way of learning is just the opposite of that of an S. Rather than relying mostly on your five senses, your approach to learning is driven by your "sixth" sense, your intuition. You are a curious person who loves challenges and hates repetition. When you are given an assignment, you want the freedom to be creative, and even if you are given specific directions, you may not follow them, preferring to be original in your approach. In your writing, you tend to generalize because you assume your readers can fill in the specific details for themselves. Likewise, you tend to respond to people's questions in general terms, and you cannot understand why others (particularly the Ss) push you to be more specific. You may be accused of being absentminded because you enjoy contemplating several ideas at once. You enjoy the creativity of word games and clever puns. You think positively and are driven by future concerns. You are sometimes impractical: You might fantasize about spending your imaginary lottery winnings rather than focusing on paying today's bills. Unlike the Sensor, you are happy when you can find the connections or meanings behind things. Rather than accepting what is, you tend to wonder what could be.

Once again, you probably saw characteristics of both the Sensing and the iNtuitve types in yourself. One preference, however, is more predominant than the other. Check *one* of the following:

I am primarily an S _____, or I am primarily an N _____.

Thinkers and Feelers

The categories of Thinking (T) and Feeling (F) relate to how people are most apt to arrive at their decisions. The names of these categories should not be taken too literally. People who are predominantly Feeling *do* think, and people who are predominantly Thinking have feelings for others. However, when it comes to making a decision, one or the other preference, T or F, influences our choices.

If you are a *Thinking* person, your decisions are usually based on what you consider to be right, fair, and truthful. Because you evaluate with your head and not your heart and love to analyze situations, you appear to be cool, calm, collected, and perhaps even calculating. When you are writing, you tend to be logical, precise, and to the point. However, when you write, you may forget to consider your reading audience because you assume that everyone thinks the way you do. When working in a group, you may be considered strong-minded or overbearing because you have no trouble telling people who disagree with you what you believe to be true. Your presentations follow a strict and orderly plan, and you expect that logical organization in others' presentations. You are interested in ideas that can be proven reasonably or scientifically. You are capable of making tough decisions because you focus on what you believe to be right, even though someone else's feelings might be hurt.

If you are a *Feeling* person, you are usually very conscious of the emotional reactions of others and base your decisions on what will make people happy. Because you are such a sensitive person, you may take others' comments and actions a little too personally, and therefore your own feelings may be easily hurt. You prefer peace and harmony even if you must compromise. In written assignments and oral presentations, you are strongly aware of your audience. You develop ideas by referring to your own feelings and those of others. Sometimes Fs are talkative in group discussions. This talkativeness stems from the need to include all group members in the discussion. You strive to make others content and believe that the best decisions are those that accommodate the feelings of others.

From reading about the decision-making processes of Thinkers and Feelers, you may now identify your major method for making decisions. If you are more concerned about right and wrong and logical conclusions, you are primarily a T. If you are more concerned with how your decisions will affect those involved, you are primarily an F. Check *one* of the following:

I am primarily a T _____, or I am primarily an F _____.

Judgers and Perceivers

The last two opposites, Judging (J) and Perceiving (P), relate to your approaches to work and play. If you prefer to live in a relatively organized and structured way, you are a J, but if you tend to be more spontaneous and flexible, you are probably a P.

If you are a *Judger*, you appreciate and need organization in your life. You like to be on time, meet deadlines, and have closure; in other words, you like to be in control and don't like to leave anything unfinished. Therefore, when you write, you are usually well organized, but you may not fully develop the writing assignment because you are too anxious to finish it. If you work in a group, you want everyone to keep on track. You like keeping lists and knowing what you are going to do in advance. You are a productive worker and do not appreciate interruptions. When driving home from work or school, you habitually choose the same route. Last-minute changes are not welcome. In fact, you might plan next summer's vacation in the winter. You manage your time well and almost always do any work that needs to be done before playing. Sometimes you never find the time to play.

If you are a *Perceiver*, you are much more spontaneous than a Judger. You are creative and adapt well to changing situations. Because your thinking and writing are often spontaneous, your first drafts tend to be disorganized, so you may need to do lots of revising. Also, because you are always looking for more information, you have a difficult time finishing assignments or coming to closure. If you work in a group, you may frequently get off the subject. To you, as a P, each topic has so many interesting aspects that you cannot limit yourself to one; you have a need to explore them all. You usually keep lists or schedules only in your head, but if you do write one out, it is much too long and involved and usually ends up being trashed or lost. You often act on the spur of the moment, enjoy surprises, and are easily distracted. When you are driving to or from work or school, you may explore alternative routes just for the fun of it. You often find yourself finishing a task or even starting one at the last minute. You prefer playing to working and often turn work into play.

These opposites, Judging and Perceiving, indicate how much structure you prefer in your life. Often both Js and Ps are forced to compromise because of people or situations at home, at work, or at school. Thus, you may want to consider the following situation to determine if you tend to be a J or a P: Suppose you were independently wealthy, retired, or in some other way responsible only for yourself. Which description best fits the way you would live? A J prefers living an organized, scheduled, predictable life, whereas a P prefers living a spontaneous, flexible life, where time and structure are of little importance. Check *one* of the following:

I am primarily a J _____, or I am primarily a P _____.

Your Personality Type

Your personality type is a combination of your four preferences from the descriptions above. Look back at the letters you checked, and write those four letters in the blanks below to identify your preferred personality type.

E or I	S or N	T or F	J or P
_____	_____	_____	_____

These four letters indicate one of the sixteen MBTI personality types.

Understanding MBTI Types

According to the MBTI, when the four pairs of opposite characteristics are arranged in all possible combinations, sixteen different types exist. No one type is better, or for that matter worse, than any other type. They are all merely different. People of the same type will share similar characteristics. However, people of the same type may be very different because the degree of preference in each of the four categories could fluctuate greatly from one individual to another. The following illustration will help you understand the concept: Just because a number of people enjoy rock concerts doesn't mean that they all go to the same concerts or like the same singers, the same songs, or the same instruments. In a similar sense, you *do* have a personality type that you share with others of the same type, but you are still unique as an individual.

Once you have determined your type, you can explore the characteristics of each of the sixteen different types, which are described in the next few pages, and consider the significance of knowing why people behave and react differently. As you read the type descriptions, you may find yourself saying, "Boy, does that ever sound like me," or "This type describes my best friend to a T!" or "Parts of this type were obviously written about my mother!" Certainly you will recognize your own and other people's descriptions.

Sometimes you may have had no difficulty in determining your preferences in one or more categories; however, you had trouble choosing a preference from a given pair of opposites. For instance, you may be relatively certain about three letters of your type: E_FJ, for example. However, when you take in information, you are not sure whether you are a Sensor (S) or an iNtuitive (N). In this case, read both the ESFJ and the ENFJ type descriptions. You will probably find that you identify with one type as a whole more than you do with the other. Whatever type describes you most closely, keep in mind that *each type is good* and contributes essential diversity to society. In other words, whoever you are, you're okay.

Reference Section: The Sixteen MBTI Profiles

The following descriptions can serve as a reference for you.

ISTJ types have a strong sense of responsibility. Although they are generally quiet, private, and reserved, many have excellent interpersonal skills, but they expect a bottom-line, no-nonsense response from others. They are organized, practical, and self-reliant, having the ability to get things done without being distracted.

ISTP types are very similar to ISTJ types except that they are more versatile and spontaneous. They are objective and tend to wait and see what is going to happen. They are interested in cause and effect, may be mechanically inclined, and often enjoy participating in sports. They are keenly observant and analytical and like to organize facts logically. Their quiet sense of humor is an endearing quality.

ISFJ types are usually very concerned about the feelings of others, and they do everything in their power to help others. They are good with details, facts, and figures and have a strong sense of duty. They have perseverance and are very responsible, meticulous, and conscientious. They are loyal friends.

ISFP types are tolerant unless one of their inner values is compromised. They thrive on harmony. They care about others deeply, but they usually show their feelings by their actions, not their words. They tend to avoid being leaders, but they are loyal followers, usually rather modest about their achievements. They enjoy starting many projects. They are quiet but friendly. They get what needs to be done accomplished but do not like to be rushed.

INFJ types are quietly efficient and are great problem solvers. They enjoy being creative and tend to generate many new ideas. They value harmony and seek the approval of others. They have very strong convictions based on their personal values. They put effort into what they do and feel a need to serve humanity in a useful, orderly way. The future and future plans are more important than the present.

INFP types are idealistic and true to their personal convictions. They enjoy learning, especially manipulating oral or written language. They like new ideas. They prefer working alone, and although they are friendly, being sociable is not very important to them. They have a tendency to take on more than they can reasonably accomplish. They are more concerned with helping others than with collecting possessions or controlling their surroundings. Once they accept you as a friend, you are a friend for life. They are flexible and enjoy doing things on the spur of the moment.

INTJ types are self-reliant and often act independently of authority. They value knowledge and competence. They are analytical and often skeptical. They are self-motivated and have good organizational skills. They are always looking for ways to improve practically everything and can be very determined. They are quiet, forceful leaders. Their daring intuition and insights make them see the big picture.

INTP types are more interested in ideas than in people. They have a thirst for knowledge for its own sake rather than for practical uses or human concerns. They tend to be quiet people who dislike large parties and small talk. They are introspective and like using logic and analysis to solve problems. They often do well in theoretical or scientific areas. They are flexible and open-minded concerning new ideas and possibilities. Sometimes other types have difficulty following INTPs' complex, abstract reasoning.

ESTP types are realistic and live for the moment. They are action-oriented people who want to be moving and doing instead of pondering and planning. They like hands-on tasks and would rather assemble a project on their own than read the directions or listen to explanations. When faced with problems, they work quickly to solve them. They tend not to be worriers. Socially, they have many friends and are openly accepting of others and themselves.

ESTJ types are realistic as well as practical. They have a high regard for organization, efficiency, scheduling, projects, data, and decision making. They are determined and tough-minded. Their interest lies more with the task than with the people around them. They make good administrators as long as they can remember to think about the views and feelings of others.

ESFP types are flamboyant, fun-loving people who savor the present, often to the exclusion of the past or future. They have many, many friends and will go out of their way to help them. Because they like people and physical movement, they love attending parties and participating in sports and/or exercising. They would rather work with facts than with theories, and they provide strength and support in practical situations because of their common-sense approach.

ESFJ types bring harmony to almost any situation or occasion and become upset by conflict. Because of their warmheartedness, sympathy, talkativeness, and caring ways, they make everyone feel at home and comfortable. They place others' needs before their own. They are popular people, and they work well with others and make good group members because of their dedication and their ability to organize and structure situations.

ENFP types have the same warm, outgoing personalities as the ESFJs, but they also are vivacious and imaginative. They are very good at dealing with people or situations because of their enthusiasm, their persuasiveness, and their ability to find on-the-spot solutions. They are open to new ideas and are capable of doing almost anything they are interested in doing. Sometimes, however, because of their varied interests, they may get bored in the middle of a project. They are people-oriented, striving for understanding without criticism.

ENFJ types are often leaders. Their tact and fluent speaking ability make them very persuasive. They are comfortable at leading group discussions and are acutely aware of others' feelings, needs, and contributions. They are innovative and future-oriented, with strong organizational skills, but they seldom lose sight of how their plans and decisions will affect other people. They encourage camaraderie among others and are usually popular and sociable.

ENTP types tend to have many interests and abilities and to process information quickly. Because they speak knowledgeably about many subjects and are challenged by the logic of controversy, they will argue either side of an issue—just for the sake of argument. They are excellent problem solvers, but dislike doing routine tasks. Their fascination with fresh ideas may constantly lead them in new directions, but they are adept at logically explaining these changes of focus. They are noticeable because they are energetic, enthusiastic, and animated.

ENTJ types prefer to be leaders because they like to be in control of themselves, others, and all situations. They have great confidence, persuasiveness, and enthusiasm, and they want their opinions known on any topic being discussed. Their vision of the future usually results in long-range plans that include concrete organizational plans or products. They are powerful people who direct their energies to the outside world and its endless possibilities.

MBTI in the Classroom

In the classroom, Extraverted and Introverted students behave differently. Extraverts may respond quickly and vocally and enjoy working in groups. Introverts, on the other hand, take time to rehearse their answers silently and may seldom or never respond aloud, and they usually prefer working alone. The way you use your natural E or I preference may influence your rapport with your instructor and may even affect your grade. If class participation is a part of your grade, you need to participate actively regardless of your comfort level. Extraverts, who outnumber Introverts in the general population, should make a special effort to listen and not to monopolize class discussions. Introverts, on the other hand, could risk answering and asking questions more often.

Differences also exist in the classroom for the second category, Sensors and iNtuitives. Sensors like to have step-by-step directions, with everything spelled out for them in detail. INtuitive students do not need sequential directions and prefer more open-ended assignments. For a Sensing student, an iNtuitive instructor may seem to jump from one idea to another, start with the big picture, and assume that everyone will pick up the details. For an iNtuitive student, the Sensing teacher may seem to dwell on specific details and endless facts and never get to the important or major point. The following two scenarios illustrate the different responses by Sensing (S) and iNtuitive (N) students.

Suppose you are in a class where the instructor assigns a research project with only the following directions: "Do whatever seems valuable to you. Just make sure you turn it in the week before finals." An N's response to this assignment might be, "Oh, neat! I've got a couple of ideas about the topic already. This will be easy." However, an S would be internally generating a thousand questions: "What do you mean by project? Should it be a written report? Oral? How long should it be? What format do you want?" The N prefers latitude and lots of room for creativity, whereas the S prefers much more specific details and instructions.

On the other hand, suppose the instructor said, "I want you to write a ten-page, typewritten, double-spaced report on the results of the Civil War on the South, using no more and no less than six sources (four books and two magazines), and be sure you turn it in before class on Monday of the week before finals." The S would feel comfortable with the assignment because the steps are clearly laid out, but the N would now probably feel frustrated and stifled.

An S in an N's classroom must gain structure by being thoroughly prepared before class and by meticulously editing his or her notes and perhaps even outlining notes and the text after class to make the material completely understandable. These students should also ask for clarification, more details, or examples. The N in an S's class needs to respect the instructor's knowledge, be tolerant of the lecture style, and understand that approximately 70 percent of the students are Ss and need to have all the details laid out. Ns can use this time to make mental connections and think about the topic as a whole. In terms of assignments, an N student could try to negotiate for some flexibility, or be realistic and say, "Okay, if that's the assignment, that's what I have to do."

Knowing how you prefer to learn or take in information is not going to change the way assignments are given or the way individual instructors teach. However, this awareness of MBTI types will allow you to understand your preferences, cope with your frustrations, and adapt to your classroom situation in a positive way.

The third set of opposites, Thinkers and Feelers, arrive at decisions differently. These differences, too, have an impact on learning. Thinking types base their decisions on logic and what they perceive as right and wrong. Feeling types base their decisions on personal values and their perception of how others will be affected. Sometimes conflicts between instructors and students can occur when Thinking and Feeling types are trying to communicate. T instructors tend to be more direct and to the point, wanting students to respond in a matter-of-fact way. F instructors tend to lavish praise and prefer students' personal responses. In a situation, for example, in which an F student is trying to resolve an issue with a T instructor, the student would be wise to use objective and logical reasons rather than subjective and emotional language.

The fourth area of differences in the classroom involves the Judging and Perceiving types. Judgers are well-organized, time-conscious people who like to keep schedules and lists. Their preference for structured environments allows them to fit comfortably into most academic situations. Perceivers, however, are more spontaneous and flexible and are not as concerned with time. They may often prefer leaving completion of tasks until the last minute. Both types, but especially Perceivers, however, must realize that reading comprehension, writing, thinking, and storing information in long-term memory *all* require *time*.

Knowing your MBTI personality type and preferences will allow you to understand yourself and others better, to use your preferences as strengths in learning situations, and to realize that sometimes you may choose to work outside your preference.

Summary

In this chapter, you learned information about yourself that can make you a more powerful learner.

First of all, using your peak time, that time of day when you are most mentally and physically alert, can be useful. If possible, take your most difficult classes or study your most challenging courses at your peak time.

Next, you discovered your preferred learning style(s): visual, learning best by seeing information; auditory, learning best by hearing information; or tactile, learning best by hands-on techniques. To get the most out of your classroom and study time, you need to capitalize on your preferred learning style, but also learn to incorporate other learning styles.

Third, you learned some ways to help keep yourself motivated. Students who have internal locus of control accept responsibility for their actions, whereas those who have external locus of control blame others. Besides taking responsibility, you need to develop a positive outlook by using positive self-talk and visualization in order to stay motivated.

Finally, you learned about the Myers-Briggs Type Indicator (MBTI), which isolates four pairs of contrasting preferences: Extravert or Introvert, which is an indication of where you get your energy; Sensing or iNtuition, which is the way you prefer to gather information; Thinking or Feeling, which indicates your preferred way of making decisions; and Judging or Perceiving, which is how you prefer to live your life. The composite of these variables creates sixteen different personality types, all of which are equally good. Knowing your type and knowing that fifteen others exist can help you deal better with yourself and others.

Chapter 6

The Power of Managing Goals, Problems, and Stress

Knowing where you want to go and how to get there is an important aspect of life. In the physical sense, knowing how to get where you want to go is rather simple. All you need is a map and some kind of transportation. In a mental sense, however, knowing where you want to go and how to get there generally requires more calculated effort. In other words, what are your goals in life, and how are you going to achieve them?

In this chapter, you will learn how to reach long-term goals by setting short-term goals. You will also learn a powerful problem-solving technique, SOLVE, for overcoming both large and small problems. Finally, you will learn to understand and manage stress better, especially as it relates to college. The techniques you will learn in this chapter will help you gain the power to manage your life better.

GOAL SETTING

A *goal* is the objective or purpose toward which an effort is directed. *Long-term goals* are large achievements that often take a significant amount of time, such as graduating from college, being accepted in your profession, buying a house, or making your first million. *Short-term goals* provide the smaller steps that you need to take in order to reach your long-term goals, such as STUDY-READING an assignment, creating an effective résumé, saving a certain amount of money every week, and making wise financial investments.

For a goal to be meaningful to you, it must have three components:

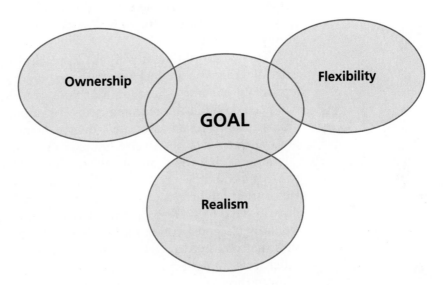

Ownership

The first criterion for a meaningful goal is that it must be something that *you* really want. Even if a relative or friend says, "This is something I think would be good for you," unless you yourself truly want to do it, it will not be your goal, but rather something you are doing to please someone else. In other words, a goal must be something that you choose for yourself and must be something that you personally value.

One way of determining if a goal is really yours is to ask yourself the following questions: Am I personally and genuinely interested in this goal? Am I willing to sacrifice other comforts and interests to achieve it? If your answers to these questions are yes, then the goal is yours, and you will probably be motivated enough to pursue it.

Realism

When you set your goals, you will need to take into consideration not only what you want, but also what you can realistically achieve. This may involve first taking an inventory of your personal talents, interests, and background. If, for example, you are twenty-five years old and have never played a musical instrument, deciding to become a concert pianist probably would be unrealistic. On the other hand, if you have studied the violin since the age of seven and have been accepted into a college of music, it would be realistic to have a long-term goal of playing in a symphony orchestra.

The length of time it will take to reach the goal must also be realistic. Whether you are seeking a two-year or a four-year degree or are in a program of some other length of time, you should plan the time *you* will need to fulfill the requirements. For example, some two-year programs leading to an associate's degree cram in as many as nineteen hours a quarter (when twelve hours is a full-time load) and require attendance during the summer. Although completing such a program in two years could be a realistic goal, you also need to weigh all the other factors that might make a two-year time frame unrealistic. For instance, do you have to work part time? Do you have family obligations that would make going to school full time difficult? Do you have prerequisites that you need to take before you start your program? These and other factors might mean that your goal would be more realistic if you allowed three, four, or even five years or more to complete your associate's degree. Whatever your goal, you need to establish a beginning point and an ending point when you can say, "Yes, I've accomplished that goal."

When considering your career goals, you might want to visit the career planning and placement center at your college. It can offer you resources such as books, audiovisual materials, computer software, career testing, and career counseling. These services are usually offered to you free or with a minimal fee to cover the cost of testing materials.

As you evaluate how achievable your career goal—or any other goal, for that matter—is, you would do well to ask yourself several questions: Do I have the mental ability to accomplish this goal? Do I have the physical ability? Do I have the talent? Do I have the resources—including opportunity, time, and means (financial and other)—to accomplish it? Are there any other factors that might keep me from reaching this goal? If so, what can I do to overcome these obstacles? Being realistic does not necessarily mean that you should give up a goal. If you have the ability and the desire, you need to focus your energy on practical and creative ways to accomplish your goal.

Flexibility

Third, to have a meaningful goal, you must be flexible; that is, you must be willing to evaluate your goal continually and to revise it if necessary.

Because situations change and unforeseen obstacles arise, you must be prepared to face these possibilities realistically and then make whatever adjustments are needed in order to reach your goal.

Although it is important to establish a time for completing your goal, if some significant problem arises that sets you back, you do not need to abandon your goal, but you may need to revise your timetable. For example, suppose your old, reliable car finally gives out on you. It cannot be repaired, and if you buy another car, even a used car, you won't have enough money for tuition the following term. This might mean that you would have to drop out of school for a while to earn enough money to buy the car. This setback, however discouraging, does not mean you have to quit college completely, but it does mean you have to adjust your time frame.

Short-Term Goals to Long-Term Goals

Long-term goals by their very nature often seem far away and beyond reach. The means of reaching a long-term goal, therefore, may seem monumental. For example, if you are just beginning college and are planning to become a doctor, having to complete four years of undergraduate school, three years of medical school, and another three years of internship and residency may seem impossibly demanding. However,

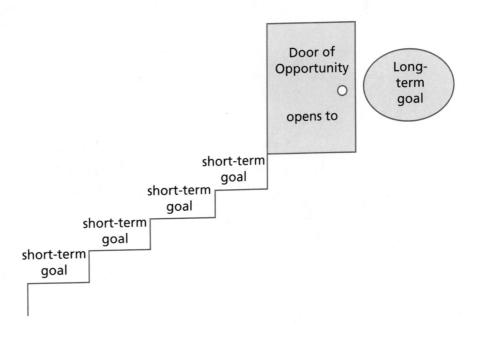

by setting short-term goals, you can gradually work your way up to achieving your long-term goal, even one as far away as ten years from now. Completing an assignment, completing a course, and completing a term of classes may be considered short-term goals because they can be accomplished in the foreseeable future.

Short-term goals by definition are smaller, more immediate, and more readily attainable than long-term goals. Therefore, in order to stay motivated and to encourage yourself along the way, you need to

Exercise 6-A

Directions: Choose one course you are taking. Write one long-term goal for that course. Then write five short-term goals that you can use to reach the long-term goal. Be prepared to discuss your list of goals in class.

Course: _____

Long-Term Goal: _____

_____

Short-Term Goals:

1. _____

_____

2. _____

_____

3. _____

_____

4. _____

_____

5. _____

_____

focus on short-term goals that you can meet within a month, a week, a day, or even a class period. Each short-term goal that is completed builds confidence and, like climbing the steps of a staircase, brings you closer to reaching your long-term goal. In order for short-term goals to be effective, you must make sure they are very specific and action-oriented. For example, instead of stating, "I will study harder," you need to identify specific actions, such as, "I will work 10 math problems every day even if they are not assigned" and "I will go to the math lab to work with a tutor on Monday and Wednesday for an hour after English class."

PROBLEM SOLVING

If you are like most people, when you set short-term and long-term goals for yourself, you probably assume that everything will go according to plan. However, as you read in the section on flexibility, the best-made plans may sometimes go awry when problems interfere. An integral part of setting and achieving goals is being able to overcome problems.

Everyone has problems. Some are simple, like what to wear or where to go for lunch. Others are more complex, like how to finance a college education, what to choose as a major, or, in your personal life, whether or not to get married or divorced. Instinctively, almost everyone uses some method for solving problems. However, some of these methods may be more effective than others.

One ineffective approach to solving problems may be described as *reactive:* You just sit back and take a wait-and-see attitude, hoping that the problem will go away or that somebody else will rescue you. On occasion, such inaction may work; however, you run a distinct risk of being mowed down while you wait to see what develops. Your lack of action might even make the problem worse.

A second, more powerful means of solving problems is the proactive approach. *Proactive problem solvers* recognize when situations are getting out of hand. Instead of sticking their heads in the sand, they act in a timely way, approaching the problem directly and logically, and trying to alleviate possible negative, painful, or embarrassing consequences.

Once you develop a systematic way to solve your problems, you, too, can approach your problems proactively. A five-step proactive way to *SOLVE* problems is illustrated below:

S = *Search out* the *real* problem
O = *Open* your mind to *all* options
L = *Line up* your plan of action
V = *Venture* upon your plan
E = *Evaluate* the results

Search Out the Real Problem

What your true problem is may seem self-evident. But often you, like many other people, may deceive yourself. For example, if you are not doing well in a class, you might say, "I'm not getting good grades because the teacher doesn't like me." Chances are that this is just an excuse and not the real reason your grades are poor. More probable reasons may involve your own behavior.

By searching out the real problem through a series of questions, you are better able to assess the situation. Are you studying as much as you should? Do you dislike the teacher, and are you using that negative attitude as an excuse? Do you lack the educational background or experience to do well in the class? Whatever the problem, you need to be honest with yourself in order to identify the real problem.

If you have trouble thinking in terms of questions, you may want to focus on five basic questions:

- *Who:* Who is involved?
- *When:* When do I feel the impact of the problem the most?
- *Where:* Where am I when the problem occurs?
- *Why:* Why do I feel defeated in this endeavor?

Eventually, you will search out the major cause or causes of the problem:

- *What:* What is my *real* problem?

Exercise 6-B

Directions: **Search out the *real* problem.** On a piece of summary paper, write down a problem you are having at work, at school, or at home that you need to solve. Then ask and answer questions, including *who, when, where,* and *why,* in writing. Finally, ask the important *what* question that will identify your real problem.

Open Your Mind to All Options

Once you have searched out the real problem, your second step is to open your mind to all options by brainstorming all the possibilities available for solving that problem. *Brainstorming* entails jotting down a list of possible solutions without being judgmental. In other words, while you are brainstorming, do not inhibit yourself by trying to decide whether an idea is silly, dumb, unworkable, okay, or even great. Simply write down everything and anything that comes to mind until you think you have exhausted all possibilities.

In the process of brainstorming, you might even find it especially useful to have a friend help you think of ideas because that is a good way to come up with as many options as possible. You may be too close to the problem to see all the options. The other person may offer additional ideas that you would never have thought of yourself. The more possible solutions you identify, the better chance you have of finding a workable one.

Exercise 6-C

Directions: **Open your mind to *all* options.** Using the problem you described in Exercise 6-B, on the same piece of paper brainstorm at least ten possible solutions. Remember, do not be judgmental as you make your list.

Line Up Your Plan of Action

Once you have brainstormed your options, you are ready to consider the value of each. In this third step of the problem-solving process, lining up a plan of action, you begin by weeding out the options that seem silly or unlikely to work. Those that remain are your best possible solutions. At this point, assuming that you have more than one solution, you should prioritize what remains on your list and select one action or a combination of actions that will serve as an appropriate plan for solving your problem.

Finally, in order to make a firm commitment to yourself, write out your plan of action, including a realistic time to begin and to complete each step. Start with "I will" statements that indicate the steps you plan to take and when you plan to take them. Actually writing out your plan will help you get motivated and be firmly committed. Keep this written statement handy so that you can check your progress daily and maintain your high motivation.

Exercise 6-D

Directions: **Line up your plan of action**. Select the best option(s) from your list in Exercise 6-C, and line up your plan of action by writing "I will _____" statements. Include a time to begin and end each step.

Venture Upon Your Plan

Now you are ready to take action—to venture upon your plan. Tackle the first step, no matter how small it is, today, for as you know, tomorrow never comes. Even if that step is just making a phone call or seeking information, actually *starting* the process is the important part.

Exercise 6-E

Directions: **Venture upon your plan**. Take the first step in your solution, and then continue to follow your plan of action. Keep a written record of what you do, including dates.

Evaluate the Results

Finally, once you have acted upon and completed your plan, you have to evaluate how successful it was. You may have done this along the way to adjust for setbacks or changes, but it is essential that you evaluate the whole process once it is finished. If your plan solved your problem, congratulations; the process is completed. If your plan didn't solve the problem to your satisfaction, you need to analyze why it did not work. Then you will have to back up a little, repeating Steps 2 and 3 to devise and enact a new plan.

Regardless of the size of your problem, the SOLVE method is an effective approach because it employs basic critical thinking skills. Using SOLVE will give you the power to overcome your problems in an objective, methodical, and logical way.

Exercise 6-F

Directions: **Evaluate the results**. Once you have completed your plan of action, evaluate the results in a paragraph. If you were successful, wonderful! If not, reconsider your options and write another plan of action.

MANAGING STRESS IN COLLEGE

Even with clear goals and a proactive approach to problem solving, you, as a college student, will sometimes feel the uncomfortable pressures of stress. Most people think of stress as a negative factor in their lives. However, believe it or not, stress is a natural and necessary part of everyone's life. Or, thinking about it another way, if no one ever felt any pressure or stress, little or nothing would ever get accomplished!

Stress is an emotional, psychological, or physical reaction to a disruptive situation. As such, it can be good and healthy, a driving force that helps you get things done and live up to your own or others' expectations. Positive stress is the adrenaline surge that great athletes experience—what might give them their "winning edge." Or it can be likened to the personal magnetism of great singers, speakers, and performers when they work their audiences—what their fans would call charisma. For you the student, positive stress can help you keep your college learning on course by helping you keep up with assignments and set personal study goals. Positive stress may also allow you to compete with yourself to do your best when you take a test or exam.

On the flip side, negative stress can affect you in a bad way, both physically and mentally. Stress that lasts too long or that causes you to feel so helpless that it hinders you from performing well can take its toll. Usually this kind of debilitating stress will express itself in physical ways.

Some physical symptoms that may indicate that you are under too much stress include:

- Tightness in neck, shoulders, or back
- Trouble falling asleep or staying asleep
- Irritability, anger, and short-tempered reactions
- Headaches
- Frequent illnesses, such as colds or the flu
- Stomach and intestinal upsets
- Butterflies in the stomach
- Poor concentration
- Depression
- Overeating or undereating
- Nervous tics
- Accelerated heart rate
- Elevated blood pressure
- Escape through alcohol or other drugs

Many students who are entering college for the first time find that college itself creates its own kind of stress. If you are a recent high school

graduate, college may represent the very first time you are fully and completely on your own. While initially that may sound wonderful, along with this new-found freedom come all the responsibilities of adulthood. Although your parents may back you emotionally and maybe even financially, you realize that now your decisions and success in college are in your hands.

On the other hand, if you have been out of school for several years, you may feel a different kind of stress stemming from a lack of confidence. When you think of competing with recent high school graduates, you may feel that your education is outdated. You may even imagine that your ability to learn may have mysteriously evaporated over the years. Whether you are just out of high school or a returning student, you may find yourself showing some of the symptoms of negative stress.

Now that you know a few of the symptoms and some of the causes of stress, you can begin looking at ways to reduce or eliminate negative stress.

The root of most stress-related problems seems to be a feeling of loss of control over one's life. If this is the case, and it usually is, the general cures for stress must be control-related. Here are some general guidelines for better controlling your negative stress in college:

- Get and stay organized in your studies.
- Faithfully use proven time management techniques, especially scheduling (see Chapter 7).
- Start all projects early, allowing for a crisis or two; if there are none, you will certainly meet your deadlines.

- Realize that studying for a given course begins on day one and that reviews should be a regular daily activity.
- Understand that the desire to procrastinate is normal for most people, but it is childish to play such a risky game with your education.
- Ask for help and cooperation from other members of your family; explain that college is a commitment, not a hobby.
- Talk to your professors if you have concerns or need additional information or help.
- Don't try to do everything alone: Seek out the student support services available on campus (for example, tutoring, writing lab, math lab, test review services, career counselors, your academic adviser, the financial aid office, learning needs counselors, special interest support groups, and so on).
- Understand that you may have to say "no" sometimes, but your family, loved ones, and friends should still be a significant part of your life.
- Realize that if you are a parent, you will have to put your children's needs first and perhaps take college at a slower pace.
- Put test scores into perspective; they are not a measure of your self-worth.
- Remember that test anxiety is a learned response and can be unlearned (see Chapter 10).
- Make it a habit to use positive self-talk when your confidence is in a slump.
- Make sure your schedule includes some free time for yourself every day to do whatever you want to do.
- Eat well-balanced meals; the healthy body/healthy mind connection is genuine.
- Make exercise a part of your daily routine, even if that means parking in the farthest parking spot in order to walk a regular distance each day.
- Remind yourself of your goals.
- Find somebody to talk to; a good listener can help relieve your stress.
- Delegate routine tasks to others.
- Learn and use deep breathing and other relaxation techniques.

Exercise 6-G

This relaxation exercise, devised by Herbert Benson, M.D., author of *The Relaxation Response,* flicks "the switch that turns off tension and turns on physical and mental peace" (Faelten and Diamond 253–254).

(continued on next page)

Exercise 6-G (continued)

1. Once or twice a day, sit comfortably in a quiet place and close your eyes.
2. Deeply relax all your muscles, beginning at your feet and working up to your face. Keep your muscles relaxed.
3. Breathe naturally through your nose and become aware of your breathing. As you exhale, silently say to yourself the word "one" (or another word of your choosing).
4. Maintain a passive attitude. Don't worry about whether you're achieving a state of deep relaxation. Let relaxation come to you. When distracting thoughts enter your mind, try not to dwell on them. Instead, return to your word. Dr. Benson emphasizes that this passive attitude is perhaps the most important element in bringing on the Relaxation Response.
5. Continue for ten to twenty minutes. You may open your eyes to check the time, but don't use an alarm clock. After you finish, sit quietly with your eyes closed for a few moments. Then open your eyes and sit still for a few more minutes before you stand up.

You may make your college experience a more positive one by using the preceding guidelines for relieving stress.

Summary

In this chapter, "The Power of Managing Goals, Problems, and Stress," you examined three valuable means for keeping your life on course. After separating short-term goals from long-term goals and understanding how they relate to each other, you learned how to identify meaningful goals. Meaningful goals have three basic criteria: ownership, realism, and flexibility.

A second major consideration is problem solving. By applying the steps in SOLVE, you can logically tackle problems, however large or small. The five steps of SOLVE are:

- Search out the *real* problem.
- Open your mind to *all* options.
- Line up your plan of action.
- Venture upon your plan.
- Evaluate the results.

The third related factor is learning to manage your stress level. This includes recognizing the signs of negative stress and, more importantly, taking steps to relieve it.

By setting clear goals, dealing with your problems in an objective and logical way, and managing your personal stress, you will be better able to take powerful control of your life.

Chapter 7

The Power of Time Management

One of the popular misconceptions about college is that success depends solely upon intelligence. Certainly brain power is necessary, but you do not have to be a genius to do well in college. You do, however, need to know how to study and how to budget your time.

Walter Pauk, one of the earliest college study skills experts, states in *How to Study in College,* "Your success or failure in college depends directly upon your use of time" (35). Your success depends upon your *wise* use of time, and your lack of success could relate directly to your poor use of time.

This chapter will focus on how to be realistic about the time you have so that you can plan adequate time to study, go to classes, work, eat, sleep, live, and even have fun. Since procrastination afflicts all students (actually, almost all people), it will receive special attention—later in the chapter, of course.

REALITY CHECK

Often you may catch yourself saying, "I don't know where the day has gone." Yet each day has twenty-four hours, no more, no less. Time—you can't buy it, you can't sell it, and you can't inherit it. So do the following exercise to gain some insights into how you use your time.

Once you have completed Exercise 7-A, you can begin to assess your results.

Exercise 7-A

Directions: Approximate the number of *hours per week* you spend engaging in the following activities:

1. Eating meals _____
2. Sleeping _____
3. Attending classes and labs _____
4. Studying _____
5. Working (job outside the home) _____
6. Working at home (laundry, fixing meals, cleaning, etc.) _____
7. Driving to school and work _____
8. Keeping appointments (doctor, dentist, haircut, etc.) _____
9. Watching TV, reading, listening to music, relaxing _____
10. Exercising _____
11. Attending religious services and/or other meetings _____
12. Showering, dressing _____
13. Socializing or talking on the phone _____
14. Taking care of children _____
15. Fulfilling other responsibilities _____

Total _____

A week has 168 hours. If the total number of hours you identified in Exercise 7-A was less than 168, then either you have good control of your time and obligations *or* you may be underestimating the amount of time necessary to fulfill all your responsibilities.

If the number of hours you identified in Exercise 7-A totaled more than 168, it is time for you either to clone yourself or to reassess your priorities. You cannot realistically duplicate yourself, and you cannot do the work of one and a half or two people. If you try to overextend yourself, you may pay for it in some significant way. Your body may rebel in the only way it knows how: by getting sick. Or you may be forced to neglect something, such as your studies, your job, or your family.

Being realistic about how much time you have is important. In high school, every hour of your school day is structured for you with classes, study hours, and other activities. In college, however, although your classes are scheduled, you are responsible for determining when and how much you study. The rule of thumb for study time is that for every hour you spend in class or lab per week, you need to spend *twice* that amount of time *studying and doing homework* outside of class. For example, if you are in class twelve hours a week, then you should be studying approximately twenty-four hours a week. This means that you will be devoting thirty-six hours a week, which is equivalent to a full-time job, to meeting your college obligations. If you are taking a particularly difficult subject, you may have to allow for more study time than the ratio of two to one. Therefore, if you want to go to school full time, logically you may not be able to work full time. Likewise, if you have many family obligations, a full-time class load may not be appropriate.

Despite your best efforts to balance available time and meet your

obligations, you, like most people, may occasionally feel overwhelmed. The next part of this chapter deals with controlling time through scheduling.

SCHEDULING YOUR TIME

Schedules, calendars, checklists, planners—these are the tools of busy, successful, determined people. If you have never kept a schedule before, now is the time to learn how. Look at most successful professionals at work each day. More often than not, some kind of planner sits atop their desks to guide their daily and long-term actions and decisions. Since college is much like the professional world in its expectations of you, you should be aware of the types of schedules available so that you can use one or more, according to your needs and preferences.

Three popular types of schedules are:

1. A *time planner,* which gives you a broad overview of the whole term, plus a detailed look at your activities for the week
2. A *weekly study schedule,* which indicates specific study hours for each course
3. A *daily to-do list,* which outlines all your tasks for the day

Regardless of which types of schedules you use, take a moment to determine what your set and flexible times are. *Set* times are hours when you are obligated to be in class, at work, or involved in some other fixed activity. *Flexible* times are the hours that remain, in which you can make choices about what you do. With these two different kinds of times in mind, you can begin to plan in such a way that you balance your hours attending classes, studying, working, and having time for yourself and your family.

Time Planners

To have an overview of important dates for each school term, a good place to start is with a planner, which usually takes the form of a month-at-a-glance or a week-at-a-glance. They are readily available in your college bookstore, as well as in discount stores and office supply stores. Whichever one you use, your time planner should have enough room to write down both college and personal activities. If it is updated frequently and referred to often, your time planner can serve as an invaluable tool for balancing school, family, work, and social commitments. It can also prevent the embarrassment of missing an appointment or of scheduling two activities for the same time.

To set up your time planner, copy important dates from your official school calendar. These may include such information as registration dates, tuition payment dates, holidays, last day to withdraw, and final exam week. Once you have the college dates on your planner, go through your syllabi and record all major test dates, due dates for papers, and due dates for any other major assignments. Then record such items as birthdays and various appointments or events that you will be attending. That way you can see an overview of your commitments at a glance, and you are less likely to forget when a paper is due or an appointment is scheduled. Because this planner is going to be your major scheduling tool, you need to continue adding commitments, such as additional test dates, personal appointments, conferences, or meetings, throughout the term as you become aware of them.

Exercise 7-B

Directions: If you have not already started a time planner, do so now. Your instructor may ask you to photocopy a week's worth to hand in.

Weekly Study Schedule

The second kind of time organizer is called a weekly study schedule. A completed one may look like the example on the next page.

The weekly study schedule is based on a seven-day week and is to be used in addition to the time planner.

To create a weekly study schedule, write down all your set commitments in the appropriate boxes. Then fill in the remaining boxes with your flexible activities. To make sure you include sufficient and specific study hours, use the two-for-one rule—for every hour you spend in class or lab, you need to spend two hours studying and doing homework. The major advantage of the study schedule is that it identifies specific times for studying specific courses during each day of the week.

Each weekend, make out a study schedule for the following week

Time	Sun.	Mon.	Tues.	Wed.	Thurs.	Fri.	Sat.
7-8 a.m.	sleep		dress	eat			sleep
8-9 a.m.	sleep		drive	time			sleep
9-10 a.m.		Biology	Bio	Bio	Sdy	Bio	free
10-11 a.m.	church	StSkills	lab	StSkills	Bio	SS Lab	time
11 a.m. - 12 p.m.		sty Psyc	Psyc	sty SS	Psyc	sty Psyc	gym
12-1 p.m.	eat	sty Psyc	free	sty Bio	free	sty Psyc	eat
1-2 p.m.	gym			Lunch			Eng hw
2-3 p.m.	free	English	sty Bio	Eng.	sty Psyc	Eng.	sty SS
3-4 p.m.		sty Eng	sty SS	English — essay — draft			sty Bio
4-5 p.m.				driving			sty Psyc
5-6 p.m.				dinner			
6-7 p.m.	sty Psyc			Work			
7-8 p.m.	sty Bio			Work			free time
8-9 p.m.	sty SS			Work			
9-10 p.m.	TV		driving	Gym	driving		
10-11 p.m.	Rec	sty Psyc	sty Bio	driving	sty Bio	free	
11 p.m. - 12 a.m.	read		sleep			time	

that includes all the hours from the time you get up until the time you go to bed—with some spaces designating, as they should, "relax" or "watch TV."

One easy way to keep a weekly study schedule and avoid a lot of re-writing is to write all your set activities in pen and your flexible activities in pencil. Another way is to write your set activities in the blocks of the study schedule, then insert the paper in a see-through plastic folder. Using an erasable marker, write your flexible activities on the plastic cover.

Either of these methods serves two purposes: First, if you need to change something, you can do it easily. For example, if you have decided to study from 7 to 10 P.M. on Tuesday, but someone calls to invite you to a movie you are dying to see, you can reschedule your studying for a time when you had planned to watch TV or do some other flexible activity. Just erase it and write it in somewhere else. If you adhere to your revised schedule, you will not feel guilty about going out, and you will still get the studying done that you had planned. Second, you will not need to write out a whole new schedule every week. You will have to change only the flexible times.

Another shortcut you can use to prepare a study schedule is to fill out a schedule with your set activities and then photocopy the schedule for each week of the term. Then all you have to fill in each week are the flexible activities. If you fill them in with erasable pen or pencil, you can still make minor changes as the need arises.

You can photocopy the blank weekly study schedule that appears in this chapter for your own use.

Exercise 7-C

Directions: Make two photocopies of the blank study schedule (one to keep and one to hand in), and fill in your set times and flexible times for the upcoming week. You may want to do the set times in ink and the flexible times in pencil.

Daily To-Do Lists

A daily to-do list, as its name implies, is not actually a schedule, but rather a list of tasks, assignments, errands, or projects you need to accomplish on that day. No matter what type of schedule you are using, the daily to-do list is extremely important because it is more action-oriented than the other schedules. Every evening or early in the morning, you should make a list of what needs to be accomplished during the day. You can make your list on a 3 x 5 card, on a piece of paper, or in a special

Time	Sunday	Monday	Tuesday	Wed.	Thurs.	Friday	Sat.
7-8 a.m.							
8-9 a.m.							
9-10 a.m.							
10-11 a.m.							
11 a.m. - 12 p.m.							
12-1 p.m.							
1-2 p.m.							
2-3 p.m.							
3-4 p.m.							
4-5 p.m.							
5-6 p.m.							
6-7 p.m.							
7-8 p.m.							
8-9 p.m.							
9-10 p.m.							
10-11 p.m.							
11 p.m. - 12 a.m.							

notebook—whatever works for you. Some people divide their to-do list into three sections: must, should, and would if I had time. Others divide it into A, high priority; B, important; and C, can be delayed. Or you might rank the most important three or four items on your list. Don't forget to add last-minute appointments, obligations, and items or activities you would like to do.

Read the following true story to get a sense of the value of to-do lists (Usova 23):

First Things First

One day a management consultant, Ivy Lee, called on Schwab of the Bethlehem Steel Company. Lee outlined his firm's services briefly, ending with the statement: "With our services, you'll know how to manage better."

The indignant Schwab said, "I'm managing as well now as I know how. What we need around here is not more knowing but more doing, not knowledge but action. If you can give us something to pep us up to do the things we **already know** we ought to do, I'll gladly listen to you and pay you anything you ask."

"Fine," said Lee, "I can show you something in twenty minutes that will step up your productivity at least 50 percent."

"OK," said Schwab. "I have just about that much time before I have to catch a train. What's your idea?"

Lee pulled a blank 3-by-5 card out of his pocket, handed it to Schwab, and said: "Write on this card the six most important tasks you have to do tomorrow." That took Schwab about three minutes. "Now," said Lee, "put this card in your pocket, and the first thing tomorrow morning look at the first item. Concentrate on it until it is finished. Then tackle item two in the same way, then item three. Do this until quitting time. Don't be concerned if you finish only two or three, or even if you finish only one item. You'll be working on the important ones. The others can wait. If you can't finish them all by this method, you couldn't with another method either. And without some system, you probably would not even decide which are most important.

"Spend the last five minutes of every working day making out a 'must' list for the next day's tasks. After you've convinced yourself of the worth of this system, have your men try it. Try it out as long as you wish, and then send me a check for what you think it's worth."

(continued on the next page)

First Things First (continued)

The interview lasted about twenty-five minutes. In two weeks, Schwab sent Lee a check for $25,000 — $1,000 a minute. He added a note saying the lesson was the most profitable from a money standpoint he had ever learned. Did it work? In five years it turned the unknown Bethlehem Steel Company into the biggest independent steel producer in the world, making Schwab 100 times a millionaire and the best-known steel man of that time.

Admittedly, making a daily to-do list does not mean you will become a multimillionaire as Charles Michael Schwab did, but you should be able to get done what needs to be finished every day.

If you have not made lists before and your lists tend to be much too long to accomplish, you may want to "guesstimate" how long each task will take and then write down how long it actually did take to do it. Knowing how long a given project usually takes can help you write more realistic lists.

At the end of the day, a typical to-do list, not including the student's classes or work schedule, might look like the illustration below. The two items that were not checked off can be added to the next day's to-do list.

As you complete the items on your list, you will not only have each small task accomplished, but you will also have the psychological satis-

10/16 To-Do List

- ☑ Study for biology test. Ch. 8 & 9
- ☑ Mail Visa bill
- ☑ Lunch with Carolyn 12–1—cafeteria
- ☑ Conference with Prof. Luther about Eng. paper 10:00
- ☐ Go to library to find books on W.W. II paper
- ☐ Get haircut
- ☑ Study-read Ch. 4 in Psych.
- ☑ Do 20 calculus problems

Exercise 7-D

Directions: Starting tonight or tomorrow morning, make a daily to-do list every day for the next five days (omit weekends if you choose to do so). Anything you do not accomplish during a given day, add to the following day's list. Be prepared to turn in these lists (or a photocopy).

---

faction of checking each item off as you finish it. By the end of the day, you will feel as if you have "moved mountains" as your check marks mount up and your day's tasks come under your control.

The following overview lists the highlights of each of the three types of schedules so that you can compare their uses:

Time Planner:

- Important dates from college calendar
- Major test and due dates from syllabi
- Personal records and appointments

Weekly Study Schedule:

- Set times and activities
- Study hours (two-for-one rule)
- Flexible activities

Daily To-Do List:

- Tasks
- Assignments
- Errands
- Projects

Additional Scheduling Tips

Time planners, study schedules, and daily to-do lists are the keys to getting control of your time in college. In addition to these basic tools, here are some other useful tips for scheduling your time:

- Determine which courses are easy and which are hard for you. Study your hardest subject first.

- Study your hardest course every day.
- Consider your peak time. Study for your hardest course during your most mentally and physically alert period.
- Study as soon after class as possible. Remember the Ebbinghaus Forgetting Curve, which clearly indicates that most forgetting happens immediately after hearing or reading information.
- Prioritize: What needs to be done now? Attack the most urgent task right away.
- Study dissimilar subjects back to back. For example, if you are taking sociology and psychology, study a math course in between. Or if you are taking statistics and a math course, separate these courses in your study time with English or history. On your study schedule, insert *specific subjects* to study.
- Use *distributed effort*; that is, generally do not study for longer than an hour without taking a break. If you study for sixty minutes or less, you will accomplish more because you will be more alert.
- Note due dates and allow yourself plenty of lead time to get long projects finished.

Additional Time-Bending Techniques

Even though you have only twenty-four hours to work with every day, you can sometimes bend or stretch those hours to your advantage.

- Make use of portable study materials. For example, carry with you 3 x 5 cards with terms and vocabulary or loose pages from your notebook.
- Record information on cassette tapes to use in the car.
- Use stolen moments of time to study—for example, standing in line or waiting for an appointment or class to start.
- Do two tasks at once. Everyone has routine, repetitive chores to do, such as making the bed, washing and folding clothes, mowing the lawn, or exercising. While you are engaged in these activities, let your brain work, too, by studying.
- Study in a regular place, and be sure it is equipped with everything you need: pens, paper, books, dictionary, etc. If you always study in the same place and have a well-equipped study area, you will get to work faster and have better concentration when you are there because you will develop a conditioned response. *Conditioned response* means that the habit of study will be triggered automatically when you sit down in your study environment.

- Get into the habit of using positive self-talk. Replace "I have never been good in math" with "One by one, I can do these problems." A positive attitude will actually make studying easier.
- Reward yourself when you have completed an assignment or task. Plan your rewards, whether they are large or small, in advance. Your reward could be a snack, a phone call, a break to watch TV, exercising, a trip to the mall, or whatever will help motivate you to resume working later.
- When you have finished a task or a study session, do one more small task before you stop. You might do one more math problem or prepare tomorrow's to-do list. One more item accomplished today is one less item to complete tomorrow.

PROCRASTINATION

Most people, despite their best efforts, lapse into periods of procrastination—some people now and then, some more often, and some almost all the time. *Procrastination* is the tendency to needlessly put off jobs, tasks,

or assignments. Planners, study schedules, and daily to-do lists are useful in helping you solve the problem of procrastination, but only if you *use* them after you make them. At times, the consequences of procrastination are not too serious. If you don't clean your room, it can wait another day or two. However, if you don't do your assignments before they are due, you have a more serious problem. Missing due dates in college can have serious consequences. Procrastination that jeopardizes your success or interferes with your goals must be overcome, and it *can* be if you take positive steps.

In order to overcome the habit of procrastination in school-related tasks, you first need to analyze your reasons for procrastinating.

Reasons for Procrastination

Although many reasons for procrastination exist, four of the most common ones indicate that "procrastinators finish LAST."

L	=	Lack of motivation
A	=	Afraid of failure
S	=	Start-up problems
T	=	Task is Too overwhelming

L=Lack of Motivation   One major reason some students procrastinate is that they lack the basic motivation to take control of their goals and their lives. Although goal setting (Chapter 6) and internal locus of control (Chapter 5) were discussed previously, they both deserve further mention here because they are essential to motivation and, in turn, to overcoming procrastination. Motivation may be considered the driving force that makes you act. If your motivation is weak or lacking, you may not accomplish much.

One cause of lack of motivation may be that you have not formulated your goals clearly, or at all. If your goals are unclear, reexamine your reasons for being in college. Even if your goals are fairly clear, you may be looking only at your long-term goal (for instance, getting a degree) and forgetting about the significance of focusing on several short-term goals (for example, completing a writing assignment on time, reading an assignment, or doing twenty math problems). Short-term goals are much more visible and more easily accomplished than long-term goals. They are the smaller steps that lead you ultimately to reach your larger, long-term goal.

Alternatively, your lack of motivation may be caused by your lack of internal locus of control. For example, if you are in college only because your parents want you to be here or because your friends are here, you may not be taking responsibility for your own learning. Or, as another example, if you receive an assignment from a teacher and consider it pointless and boring and do not make an attempt to do it, then you, again, might be operating on external, rather than internal, locus of control. You do not see any reason for doing the assignment, and therefore you put off doing it or do it halfheartedly and do not really learn anything. Once again you ought to reevaluate why you are in college, what your goals are, and how you can take responsibility for doing whatever needs to be done to achieve your goals. In essence, you should clarify your personal goals and take ownership of your education.

A=Afraid of Failure   A second major reason for procrastination is being afraid of failure. Procrastination caused by fear of failure is a psychological game many people play, either because they lack self-confidence or because they are perfectionists. In fact, surprisingly, perfectionists sometimes lack self-confidence because they equate achievement with self-worth. They want everything to be perfect, and so they put off challenging tasks. Whether fear of failure stems from perfectionism or simply from a basic sense of not measuring up to the task, the result is the same: The students postpone doing an assignment until it is too late to do it well or even to do it at all. Then they do not have to face the fact that they couldn't do an acceptable job. Often people will say after the fact, "Well, I could have done it, and done it well, if I'd had more time."

If you use such an excuse, you are setting yourself up for failure and creating a self-fulfilling prophesy. In other words, you fail because you have set out to fail by not living up to either your standards or the standards that have been set for you.

To overcome procrastination that stems from being afraid of failure, you have to remind yourself that you are human. You do not have to be perfect, but you need to make an honest effort to plan your time wisely in order to finish the project without using the if-only-I-had-more-time excuse. Pace yourself by using distributed effort to complete your assignments on time.

S=Start-up Problems   A third reason for procrastinating involves the problem of getting started. If you find yourself making up a long list of excuses as to why you are not ready to start a project or assignment, then you most likely fall into this category of procrastinators.

One reason for using stalling tactics is that you are not sure how to do the task. If you are not certain about what you need to do, reread the assignment carefully to analyze what you find confusing. Jot down some specific questions about what needs to be clarified. Then see or call your instructor as soon as possible to discuss your questions. Alternatively, discuss the assignment with your classmates or ask for help in the learning center or whatever facilities exist at your school—math lab, writing lab, tutor service, etc. As soon as you have learned the answers to your questions, take action. Schedule the blocks of time you will need in order to do the task, and then follow your schedule, beginning the first task right away.

Another common reason students have for not starting a task is that they are waiting for that "magic moment." This is just another delaying tactic. "I can't write until I'm inspired," a student will say. The truth is that inspiration is 90 percent perspiration. In other words, starting a task can be hard work. Of course, you should take advantage of inspiration when it comes along, but waiting for it is like waiting to win the lottery. Rather than waiting for inspiration, schedule times in your planner and daily to-do list for working on the task.

T=Task Is Too Overwhelming   A fourth reason for procrastinating involves the size or importance of the task. The key to controlling an overwhelming job is to divide it into manageable parts. A large assignment does not have to be completed all at one time. Do the task bit by bit. When you have a research paper or even an essay to write, for example, you may feel overwhelmed. To get past this feeling of panic, you might first jot down ideas or do some other prewriting task. This way, you will not have to look at a blank piece of paper. At your next sitting, instead of trying to write the introduction, which is often difficult to do, you could write the body paragraph about which you feel most confident in terms of topic or content. Keep adding to the contents until you have written a rough draft. Once the rough draft is under control, you will find that revising and polishing your work are natural outcomes. Each of these steps, too, should be budgeted into your time schedule.

Whether the project is reading a textbook chapter, doing a number of math problems, or accomplishing any other large assignment, sizing it down will make it controllable. Reading a thirty-page chapter might seem formidable; reading five pages at a time is easier. To avoid procrastination, as soon as you get any assignment, budget your time by putting specific, manageable segments of the task into your time planner and daily to-do list. Then follow your schedule until the whole task is completed.

The LAST Can Be FIRST

No one really plans to procrastinate, although at times all of us are guilty of putting things off. Like Scarlett O'Hara in *Gone with the Wind,* we say, "I'll think about that tomorrow." The problem is that tomorrow never comes. Or at best, tomorrow may be too late when you are in college. If you use the following techniques, among others, to overcome your reasons for procrastinating, then instead of being LAST, you can be someone who finishes FIRST!

> **F** = Firm up your goals
> **I** = Initiate Internal locus of control
> **R** = Replace negative with positive self-talk
> **S** = Size down your task
> **T** = Take Time management seriously

Summary

Managing your time well means being realistic about your available time and how you use it. It is essential that you adopt a method of scheduling your time so that you can accomplish everything that needs to be done without forgetting appointments or other responsibilities.

Three types of schedules available to you are the time planner, which gives you a broad overview of your whole term, plus a detailed look at your activities for the week; a weekly study schedule, which indicates specific study hours for each course; and a daily to-do list, which outlines your tasks for the day. Whatever schedules you use, begin by determining your set times, when you have fixed responsibilities, and your flexible times, when you can choose what activities to do. Once you have a schedule, *use* it.

As you create your schedules, take into account the scheduling and time-bending tips listed in this chapter. These tips will help you be more productive and time-efficient.

Finally, this chapter explains some reasons why people procrastinate and some solutions to overcoming procrastination. Procrastinators finish LAST because they Lack motivation, are Afraid of failure, have Start-up problems, or think the Task is Too overwhelming. You can change LAST to FIRST by Firming up your goals, Initiating Internal locus of control, Replacing negative with positive self-talk, Sizing down your task, and Taking Time management seriously.

Chapter 8

The Power of Memory

Everyone forgets something sometimes. And almost everyone wishes he or she could remember more. You probably already have some methods to help you remember. What do you do to jog your memory? The classic (and probably the corniest) way to remember something is to tie a string around your finger. Today Post-it Notes have become a popular means of sparking memory because they are conveniently sized and adhere to most surfaces. Some people even use the human element to help them remember: "Honey, would you remind me to tell so-and-so such-and-such when we get there?"

This chapter will show you other ways to enhance your memory power. It opens with an explanation of short-term and long-term memory, followed by an explanation of the process of remembering. The chapter then describes several well-recognized strategies to help you increase your memory power and make sense out of hard-to-learn material and "slippery" facts.

SHORT-TERM AND LONG-TERM MEMORY

All memory begins with the senses because the five senses are the channels through which all information comes. However, although you are bombarded by vast numbers of sights, sounds, touches, tastes, and smells each moment of the day, only certain impressions and information actually go into your short- or long-term memory.

Short-term memory is the ability to recall bits of information for a very brief time, usually from twenty to thirty seconds unless you make a special effort to remember the information longer. For example, if you look up an unfamiliar telephone number in the phone book, you can remember that number until you have dialed it; after that you usually forget it. You may remember more familiar items somewhat longer. For example, you are likely to remember what you wore to school yesterday, but you have probably forgotten what you wore a month ago unless the date, clothing, or occasion was memorable. These two examples illustrate that short-term memory is limited in endurance and capacity. In fact, short-term memory can store only between five and nine items at a time. Thus, we can easily learn a phone number (seven digits) or a social security number (nine digits divided into three, two, and four numbers). But to get those numbers into long-term memory, we have to use them or repeat them until they are firmly in place, and that takes time.

Long-term memory, as the name implies, is the ability to recall information days, months, and even years after you have learned it. In fact, long-term memory can last a lifetime. Unlike short-term memory, long-term memory is unlimited in its capacity to store information. Examples of items that may be in your long-term memory are your own phone number and those of your closest friends, your social security number, and the multiplication tables, which you learned in grade school. Besides items composed of numbers, you also probably have nursery rhymes, lyrics to songs and commercials, and the general rules for your favorite sporting events stored in your long-term memory. Items you are able to retrieve from your long-term memory did not get there by magic. Either you made a conscious effort to put them into long-term memory or you heard them over and over for an extended period of time, as with the McDonald's commercial. If you hear the opening words, "Two all-beef patties . . . ," you can probably finish that ditty all the way to the sesame seed bun.

THE PROCESS OF REMEMBERING

Unfortunately, in terms of memory, the human brain is not like a tape recorder or VCR: It cannot take everything in and then automatically repeat it all. Moving information from short-term to long-term memory takes both time and effort.

You might think of human memory in terms of the way a computer works. A computer actually deals with information in three stages: input, storage, and output. Input takes place when you sit down at the keyboard and enter information by pressing the right keys to create a meaningful document; at this point, the information is displayed on a screen and entered into short-term memory. Storage occurs when you want to have a more lasting record of your efforts: You enter the "Save" command and name your file. Output happens when you retrieve that information for later use: You simply open the saved document and enjoy immediate recall of the information previously saved.

Like the computer, you initially have to use your senses, your power of observation, and your curiosity so that new information can register (input). When you preview a textbook chapter, for instance, you are carefully setting up a background so that you can connect and predict and make sense of your reading. Again like the computer, your brain needs a direct "save" command in order to put information into long-term memory (storage). When you mark sections in a textbook, write questions, and recite aloud over a period of time, for example, you are making a conscious and direct effort to "save" or store information in your long-term memory. Finally, when you take a test later, you should be able to respond to the questions easily and accurately (output). You realize then that your time and hard work have paid off. The test questions prompt a quick recall of information stored in your long-term memory.

The chart on the following page is a summation of the three parts of the memory process—input, storage, and output—and learning techniques that you can use to enhance that memory process.

It is important to note that you need to expend time and put forth effort in order for information to be stored in your long-term memory. Realizing this, you can probably see why cramming has earned its bad reputation. If you cram (truly a four-letter word in this sense!), you are trying to overload the capacity of short-term memory and to do so in just a few hours. Then you magically expect to retrieve that information from long-term memory the next day. Such a procedure seldom works. In essence, it creates stress, which actually interferes with your ability to process information. Cramming is not an effective shortcut to putting information into your long-term memory.

Enhancing Your Memory Process

Input	Storage	Output
How to take in information.	How to put information into long-term memory.	How to recall information later.
1. Become more observant.	1. Make a conscious effort to remember.	1. Use positive self-talk.
2. Control distractors, if possible.	2. Use your preferred learning style.	2. Focus and concentrate on test questions.
3. Understand concepts before learning them.	3. Mark texts and take notes in class.	3. Let memory techniques act as cues for recall.
4. Use sensory learning.	4. Review and recite frequently.	4. Mentally picture your personal visual organizers.
5. Be actively curious.	5. Use memory devices.	5. Use relaxation exercises to fight stress.
6. Get ready before listening to lectures.	6. Organize material personally.	
7. Preview before reading.	7. Make your own visual organizers.	

CLASSIC MEMORY TECHNIQUES

Many people make this complaint: "I have a terrible memory. I just can't remember anything!" Such a statement is not only exaggerated, it is usually untrue. Most people's memories are not bad; they are just not as well trained as they could be. Everyone uses some memory strategies. But whatever memory devices you already use, you may want to add to the power of your memory by adopting some of the following techniques: observation, association, clustering, imaging, and mnemonics.

Observation

Much of your ability to remember hinges on careful observation. *Observation* involves a *conscious* effort to pay attention, be alert, listen attentively, and notice details. If, for example, you have ever lost track of your car in a public parking lot, it was probably because you did not make a conscious effort to pay attention or to notice landmarks. Likewise, you need to employ basic observational skills both in the classroom and in your studying before you can apply any other memory techniques. When you are listening to lectures, taking notes, and studying textbooks, you must make a conscious effort to notice and remember pertinent information. For example, when you are taking notes in class, besides recording the obvious—information on the chalkboard or an overhead transparency—you should be noticing the teacher's body language, his or her vocal emphasis, and transitions and organizational cues. Careful observation of these details allows you to determine what information is of major or minor importance and what you should emphasize in your notes, that is, what is important to remember. (Now do Exercise 8-A on the next page.)

Association

The second memory technique, learning by *association*, is based upon a simple principle: Learning something new is always easier if you can associate or connect it with something you already know. For example, if you are just beginning to use a computer, you might not understand what is meant by "windows" until you realize that windows on computers are very similar to windows in buildings: When you look into them,

Exercise 8-A

Directions: Complete this exercise on observation without looking at any of these objects or people.

1. What is the color of your toothbrush? _____

2. Where is the record button on your VCR? _____

3. What brand of refrigerator is in your kitchen? _____

4. Typically, how many rings does the teacher of this class wear? _____

5. Describe a student who sits behind you in one of your classes.

   _____

   _____

   _____

6. How many desks are there in the front of this classroom? _____

7. How many separate parking lots are there on the campus? _____

8. What is the speed limit in the college parking lot(s)? _____

9. Name and briefly describe one unusual thing you saw yesterday.

   _____

   _____

   _____

   _____

10. Name two pizza places. What are their logos or symbols?

   _____

   _____

you can see what exists in the computer and in the environment. Or, in a biology class, if you are learning about the structure of neurons in the brain, you might associate one part of the neuron, the dendrites, which grow as you learn new information, with the roots of a tree, which grow when they are watered.

When you encounter new information in, for example, a math or science course, you can often relate it to some previously learned concepts because many such courses are arranged sequentially. However, if you find new information puzzling, make an effort to associate it with information you already know, such as the previous example of associating dendrites with tree roots. You might also try to relate what you are learning in one course with what you are learning in another. For example, what you learn in a psychology class about people's behavior might help you to better understand the actions, motives, and personality of a character you are reading about in your English literature class.

A practical application of remembering by association is learning people's names. The association can be either direct or silly. For example, suppose the new nurse in your doctor's office is named Karen. You discover that she is a very helpful, caring person, so you could remember her name by thinking of her as being a *caring* (Karen) person. Also, the person at the information desk at the college is named Shirley, so you think to yourself, *surely* Shirley knows everything. These are examples of direct and logical associations. Other associations might be a bit silly, but they will still help you to remember a name. For instance, if you meet a girl named Marcia at a party, you might picture her hair crowned with big white marshmallows. Marshmallows remind you of the sound of her name, Marsh-a.

Exercise 8-B

Directions: Ask two people you don't know in this class what their names are. Try to find some way to learn those names by association.

Name 1. _____

Association: _____

_____

Name 2. _____

Association: _____

_____

Clustering

Clustering, the process of grouping a large number of ideas into sub-groups, is another handy memory device. This technique is based on the fact, mentioned earlier, that you can remember several groups of five or so items more easily than a large number of separate items. If you have thirty items to learn, try to organize them into groups. For example, you might try clustering new terms you have to learn.

Clustering can also be useful as a method for prewriting or organizing an essay or research paper. If your ideas, information, or material cannot be arranged chronologically (relating to time, from first to last) or spatially (relating to area, from top to bottom, side to side, etc.), you can cluster to find categories or groupings that will provide you with a logical method of organization.

Clustering is also useful as a study technique when you have to learn a number of items. For example, in Chapter 7, on time management, eight "Additional Scheduling Tips," are listed in random order. Here is what the original list looks like:

- Determine which courses are easy and which are hard for you. Study your hardest subject first.
- Study your hardest course every day.
- Consider your peak time. Study for your hardest course during your most mentally and physically alert period.
- Study as soon after class as possible. Remember the Ebbinghaus Forgetting Curve, which clearly indicates that most forgetting happens immediately after hearing or reading information.
- Prioritize: What needs to be done now? Attack the most urgent task right away.
- Study dissimilar subjects back to back. For example, if you are taking sociology and psychology, study a math course in between. Or if you are taking statistics and a math course, separate these courses in your study time with English or history. On your study schedule, insert *specific subjects* to study.
- Use *distributed effort;* that is, generally do not study for longer than an hour without taking a break. By studying sixty minutes or less, you will accomplish more because you are more alert.
- Note due dates and allow yourself plenty of lead time to get long projects finished.

If you were required to learn these eight tips for a test, you might clus-ter them into the following three categories:

Subject Cluster	How-To Cluster	Early-Bird Cluster
Hardest first	Dissimilar back to back	ASAP after class
Hardest every day	Distributed effort	Prioritize: first things first
Hardest at peak time		Plenty of lead time for big projects

Notice how the three clusters logically combine the information as well as condense it; both processes will make it easier to learn.

Exercise 8-C

Directions: If you had a shopping list containing the following items, determine how you could cluster them.

1. On a piece of paper, rearrange the items by clustering related items into groups.

2. Give each group a title that indicates what the items have in common.

3. Put any leftover items into a group titled "Miscellaneous."

   Your goal is to make logical groups with as few leftovers as possible (or none).

tablecloth	shoes	hammer
pocket knife	lamp	cookbook
hat	pliers	perfume
cat food	toy	pencils
sled	journal	furniture polish
tricycle	comb	locket
lemons	soap	computer disk
deck of cards	salt	paper towels

Imaging

Imaging, or using a pictorial representation of something, can be an excellent way to remember a fact, process, definition, or concept. For example, most of us know the geographical shape of Italy because its image resembles a boot. However, drawing the geographical outline of Switzerland, Italy's close neighbor to the north, would prove challenging for most people, since its shape does not easily conjure up a picture.

You may already be drawing pictures in your notebooks to reinforce ideas, definitions, or other material that you need to learn. If you have not done so yet, try this method with something that you are having trouble remembering. You do not have to be a great artist. Stick figures are fine. These pictures are for your eyes only, so however they look, you will know what the picture is supposed to represent, and the picture will be imprinted on your mind because *you* drew it!

Exercise 8-D

Directions: Select a term or concept that you need to learn for any one of your courses.

1. Name the term or concept and give its definition: _____

   _____

   _____

   _____

2. Draw a picture that will provide you with an image of the term and definition:

Mnemonics

Mnemonics is a general category of memory devices; mnemonic devices include songs, ditties, and other catchy techniques to help you remember. Mnemonic devices take the form of acronyms, made-up sentences, rhymes or songs, and physical manipulations.

Acronyms   *Acronyms* are a kind of mnemonic device formed from the first letters of items you are trying to learn. These first letters are arranged to spell a word. GREAT (Chapter 1), SOLVE (Chapter 6), and LAST and FIRST (Chapter 7) are examples of acronyms in this text. People have used acronyms for ages, but in this era of rapidly increasing information, they are becoming more and more prevalent. For example, you are all familiar with Light Amplification by Stimulated Emission of Radiation printers and Light Amplification by Stimulated Emission of Radiation surgery, but you call them laser printers and laser surgery. The acronym *laser* (originally in capital letters) and other words like *radar, sonar,* and *scuba* have become so familiar that you may forget that they are acronyms.

In college, an acronym can act as a trigger to help you remember information. For example, if you have to learn the names of the five Great Lakes, it is easy to remember HOMES—standing for Huron, Ontario, Michigan, Erie, and Superior. Likewise, some people remember the colors of the spectrum in their proper order by making each color part of the name "ROY G. BIV" (red, orange, yellow, green, blue, indigo, and violet). Another acronym that is useful to know is SAGE—a "wise" way to remember the four different kinds of context clues: synonyms, antonyms, general sense of the sentence, and examples.

Sentences   Making up sentences or phrases, either nonsensical or serious, can be an effective way of learning and remembering material. The spellings of difficult words can often be learned easily with mnemonics. For instance, saying "A Rat In The House May Eat The Ice Cream" is an easy way to teach a child how to spell *arithmetic* because the sentence is silly (making it memorable), and the first letters of the words, taken together, spell *arithmetic*. For adults, mnemonics can be applied to remember more difficult or confusing spellings. For example, do you spell attendance with an *ance* or *ence*? It's easy to remember the correct spelling if you think of attending a dAnce. Likewise, FeBRuary is a very cold month—brrrrr!

Although you have learned an acronym for the colors in the spectrum, ROY G. BIV, another way to remember the colors in order is to learn the sentence "Richard Of York Gains Battles In Vain." The first letter of each word is the same as the first letter of one of the colors. If you want to learn the Great Lakes in geographical order, west to east, instead of the random order given by HOMES, you might use the sentence mnemonic "SuperMan Hates Eating Oatmeal." A third example of a sentence mnemonic to learn the letter keys of a standard keyboard on a computer is "The quick brown fox jumped over the lazy dogs." If you type this sentence, you will have practiced using all the letter keys of the three major rows on a standard keyboard.

Sentence mnemonics can help you learn very complex information as well. For example, students in biology class have to know all the basic elements of living things. The sentence to remember is "K. P. COHN'S CaFe (has) Mighty good salt." The elements this sentence helps you remember are, in order, potassium (symbol K), phosphorus (symbol P), carbon (C), oxygen (O), hydrogen (H), nitrogen (N), sulfur (S), calcium (Ca), iron (Fe), magnesium (Mg—Mighty good), and sodium and chlorine (Na and Cl), which make up salt. (The word *has* is in parenthesis because it does not have any meaning in terms of the elements in this sentence.) Thus, by learning one sentence, you can recall the eleven elements you need to know as well as their symbols.

Jingles or Rhymes   Jingles or rhymes are popular mnemonics because they help you learn through rhythm and sound. Probably the first "learning" song you encountered was the ABC song. Another popular jingle shows how to remember which months have thirty days and which ones have thirty-one. "Thirty days hath September, April, June, and November, all the rest have thirty-one; excepting February alone, which hath but twenty-eight in fine, till leap year gives it twenty-nine."

At times, using rhymes can also help you in practical situations. If you ever have to do any maintenance around the house, such as putting a washer in a faucet, attaching a hose to a spigot, or changing a light bulb, and you are relatively inexperienced, you may wonder which way to turn the wrench, hose coupling, or bulb. Although experts know that all standard threads turn clockwise to tighten, all you need to remember is "righty/tighty and lefty/loosey."

Another rhyme that you might find useful if you are taking chemistry is "-*ate,* I ate; -*ide,* I died." This rhyme helps you remember that cyan*ates* are harmless chemicals, whereas cyan*ides* are extremely poisonous—an important distinction to know.

Physical Techniques   Physical participation can also act as a mnemonic. This can mean simply putting something in a particular place, like putting letters that need to be mailed under your car keys, or acting out a process. Instead of the "Thirty Days" poem for remembering the days in the month, perhaps you learned the knuckle method. This method names the months chronologically, counting January on the first knuckle, February in between, March on the second knuckle, April in between, etc. (Don't worry about the fact that you have one in between and one knuckle left over at the end.) Knuckle months have thirty-one days; in-between-knuckle months have thirty. Unfortunately, this method does not give you a clue about how many days are in February; you are on your own to figure that out. Nevertheless, this example illustrates that mnemonic devices can include physical components, and the more senses you use to learn something, the more easily you will learn and remember.

Although mnemonic devices made up by others can be very helpful, you may want to make up your own mnemonic devices—you will really own them, and they may be even easier to remember than devices that are provided for you.

Exercise 8-E

Directions: Create your own mnemonic device so that you can easily remember the names of the five classic memory techniques:

_____

_____

Summary

In this chapter, several aspects of memory are discussed. First, short-term and long-term memory are defined. Short-term memory lasts only about thirty seconds, whereas long-term memory can last a few months, a few years, or forever. However, getting information from short-term to long-term memory takes time and concentrated effort. Committing something to memory is a process that actually includes three stages: input, storage, and output.

Finally, several classic memory techniques are explained. These include observation, association, clustering, imaging, and mnemonics. Mnemonics, an overall term for several memory techniques, include acronyms, which are words made out of the first letters of several words or phrases; silly or sensible sentences; rhymes and jingles; and various physical techniques.

Chapter 9

The Power of Making Your Own Visual Organizers

Have you ever heard the saying, "A picture is worth a thousand words"? Although the well-known expression is a little worn out, and the number is surely exaggerated, adding pictures to words can be a powerful means of enhancing your understanding and memory.

In this chapter, you will learn ways to arrange large amounts of information so that the whole picture, a summation of the information, is visible on one or two pages. This information is usually taken from lecture notes and textbook chapters. These visual organizers use key words with simple visual connections, such as lines, arrows, or geometric symbols, to depict information that you are trying to learn. You don't have to be an artist to create them. The five major visual organizers are:

1. Topic Grids
2. Action-Reaction Arrows
3. Ts
4. Webs
5. Time Lines

GETTING A HAND ON IT: PERSONAL VISUAL ORGANIZERS

The physical mnemonic device of the hand shown on the next page should help you remember the five kinds of personal visual organizers. As you can see, each finger and the thumb represents a different visual organizer.

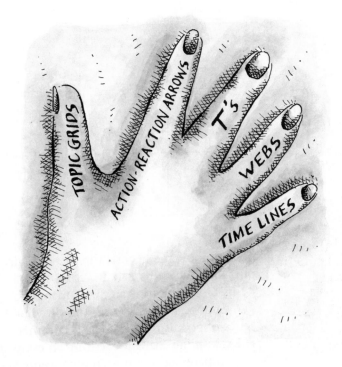

Topic Grids

Because of their concise and logical structure, topic grids provide you with a means of organizing large amounts of information. Just as the thumb allows the hand to hold and grasp many objects, the grid allows you to hold and grasp an infinite number of categories of related information. The thumb of the hand, therefore, with its ability to hold and grasp objects, is a physical mnemonic associated with the topic grid.

The topic grid, as the name implies, is made up of a series of boxes, similar to boxes on graph paper only much larger. If you have a computer with a program that generates tables and graphs, you can use this resource to create grids. Otherwise, with a ruler, you can draw a grid similar to the one illustrated on the next page. Be sure to make the boxes big enough to include all the information you need. This is the format of a typical grid before any information has been written in the boxes.

To enter information into your grid, first put the name of the general topic above the grid as the title. Next, leaving the very first box in the upper left corner empty, label each box from left to right along the top row with the name of a subdivision of this topic. Because a grid categorizes or subdivides related topics, all items across the top must be

parts of the same general topic or classification or category. This also implies that all items can be compared and contrasted. The number of items across the top can range from two to as many as to you need.

Suppose, for instance, that in your English class you are reading a series of poems related to a certain theme. These poems are being studied as a springboard for writing an essay; in your essay, you are expected to compare and contrast the concepts and poetic devices used in these poems. By creating a topic grid, you can compare and contrast the ideas within each poem, as shown in the following example:

Title: Poems About Animals

	"The Eagle" Tennyson	"Toads" Larkin	"A Bird Came Down the Walk" Dickinson	"The Tyger" Blake

Once the title and the categories are in place, you would write either questions or key words to generate information about each of the subdivisions—in this case, each of the poems—on the left-hand side of the grid going down.

When you are writing questions and statements down the side of your grid, remember that they must pertain to all the subdivisions listed across the top. In addition, you should avoid writing questions that begin with words like *does, is,* or *can,* because these lowest-level questions (see the Quality Questions Pyramid in Chapter 1) would fill the grid with yeses and noes, making it useless as a visual organizer. Here are some questions you might ask for the poetry assignment.

Title: Poems About Animals

	"The Eagle" Tennyson	"Toads" Larkin	"A Bird Came Down the Walk" Dickinson	"The Tyger" Blake
What is the tone?				
What is the theme?				
Describe the imagery.				

Now that you have identified the categories across the top and have written appropriate questions or statements down the left side, you are ready to fill in the answers to your questions for each category—here, each poem. Look at the first question (What is the tone?) and answer that question in the appropriate box under each of the poems, going across the categories. Or, if you wish, go down the grid, answering each question in the boxes under the first poem ("The Eagle"). Then continue for the other poems, one at a time. Whichever method you choose to fill in the boxes, continue writing brief answers until all the answer boxes of the grid are filled.

When writing answers in the boxes of the grid, use only key words or phrases, not complete sentences. The key words will take up less space than sentences and should jog your memory later when you are writing your essay or studying the information.

Topic grids are useful for many study situations. Whether you are studying for a test, writing an essay, or doing research for a large project, you can organize your information on a grid. Sometimes, when you are dealing with a very complex topic or have lots of sources, you may have to refer back to your sources later for additional information. If that is the case, to save time, it is a good idea to note where you obtained the information in the appropriate answer boxes by using abbreviations, such as T for textbook (with the page number), N for lecture notes (with the date), LB for library book, etc.

The following completed topic grid serves as a visual organizer for the GREAT note-taking system:

GREAT Note-Taking System

	G	R	E	A	T
What does this letter stand for?	Get ready	(w)Rite	Edit notes	Ask questions	Test yourself
When is this step used?	Before class	During class	Within 8–24 hrs. of class	Within 8–24 hrs. of class	As often as possible
How is this step done?	1. Read text 2. Review notes 3. Bring materials	1. Take notes in main column	1. Clean up	1. Generate questions in 3-in. column 2. Generate summary statement or question	1. Cover notes and answer questions out loud & in your own words 2. If wrong, restudy
Why is this step used?	1. To anticipate information from lecturer	1. To remember the lecture material 2. To have a hard copy to study from	1. To under-stand and organize info	1. To predict test questions	1. To involve sensory learning for long-term memory

Note that all the details of each step of GREAT have been carefully summarized in this one compact topic grid. In order to study from such a grid, you would simply place a piece of paper over all the grid boxes (the answers), read a statement or question, and try to recite the answer for each subdivision across the top. You can work across or down or in both directions to avoid rote memorization.

Topic grids may be useful in every college course—yes, even in math. Some students may say, "Well, I'm taking a math course, and nothing I'm learning could be put on a grid." Such an assumption is incorrect, as the following student example proves:

Topic Grid for Basic Formulas

	Rectangle	Triangle	Circle	Parallelogram
How do you find area?	$A = lw$	$A = 1/2bh$	$A = \pi r^2$	$A = bh$
What does formula mean?	Area = length times width	Area = 1/2 times base times altitude	Area = pi times radius squared	Area = base times altitude
How do you find perimeter?	$P = 2l + 2w$	$P = a + b + c$	$C = 2\pi r$	$P = 2l + 2w$
What do P formulas mean?	P = two times length plus two times width	P = side a plus side b plus side c	Circumference = 2 times pi times radius	P = two times length plus two times width
What does each variable represent?	A = area l = length w = width P = perimeter	A = area b = base h = altitude P = perimeter a, b, c = sides	A = area r = radius C = circumference	P = perimeter A = area b = base h = altitude l = length w = width
Draw an example of each.				

The beauty of a topic grid is that it consolidates and summarizes what could have been several pages of notes, as much as a whole chapter from a textbook, or a combination of both. Topic grids allow you to see relationships, similarities, and differences in the material you are learning. Studying from the grid is much more efficient than flipping back

---

Exercise 9-A

Directions: Using the directions for creating a topic grid, make a topic grid for the following information.

Ernest Hemingway, born in 1899, was a journalist and a writer of novels and short stories. When he graduated from high school in Oak Park, Illinois, he became a cub reporter on the *Kansas City Star.* He was noted for his terse prose style, which contained much dialogue. He wrote about war and his own adventures, blending realism and romanticism, and was part of the "lost generation," a group of expatriates living in Paris in the 1920s. His most ambitious novel was *For Whom the Bell Tolls* (1940). In 1953, he won the Pulitzer Prize for *The Old Man and the Sea.* He won the Nobel Prize for literature in 1954. When his physical and mental health began to fail, he shot and killed himself in 1961.

William Faulkner, born in 1897, was a humanist who explored questions of human freedom and was noted for his masterly characterizations. He wrote short stories, the most famous being "The Bear," and novels, often set in his fictitious Yoknapatawpha County, describing the regional traditions and culture of Oxford, Mississippi, Faulkner's hometown. Long, complex sentences were trademarks of his style, although he also used stream of consciousness. In the 1920s he lived in the New Orleans French Quarter with other writers and artists. He won the Nobel Prize in 1949 and the Pulitzer Prize in 1955 for *A Fable* and again in 1962 for *The Reivers.* He died in 1962.

Virginia Woolf, born in 1882, was an innovator of modern British fiction, using internal dialogue and stream of consciousness. She was educated at home, her scholarly father having an extensive library. Her best known works are *Mrs. Dalloway* and *To the Lighthouse.* In the early 1900s, she moved to Bloomsbury (a section of London) with her brother and sister, and they attracted a number of avant-garde artists, writers, and philosophers, who were known for years as the Bloomsbury Group. Besides writing novels, Woolf was famous for her critical essays. Fearing that she was going mad, she drowned herself in 1941.

through pages of notes or texts. In addition, the physical and mental act of *creating* the grid is itself a powerful learning tool. Finally, when you take a test after studying from a topic grid, that grid and all it contains will become a pictorial reference in your mind, letting you see both the overview and the details.

Action-Reaction Arrows

Action-reaction arrows are effective visual organizers when you need to show cause-and-effect relationships. Returning to our mnemonic device of the hand, just as the index finger points, so does the action-reaction diagram employ arrows to point from the direction of an action (cause) to the direction of a reaction (effect). Action-reaction arrows are adaptable to all topics that involve cause and effect because the arrows may point in any direction (up, down, kitty-cornered, etc.), to show cause-and-effect relationships.

Note how the following action-reaction arrow diagram shows the causes and effects of procrastination:

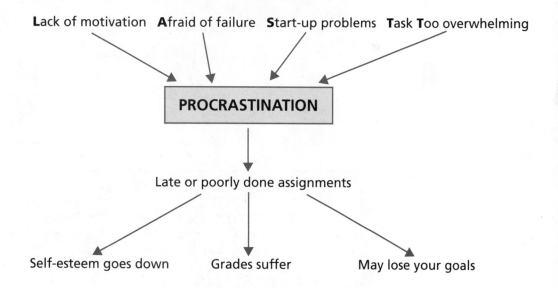

How you design your action-reaction arrows depends entirely on the complexity of the information you have. You may have one or many causes that lead to one or many effects or results. These results, in turn, might have other ramifications, which themselves become causes leading to further effects. Thus, in many instances you will have a chain reaction of cause and effect: A primary cause or causes lead to other causes and effects; these, in turn, lead to secondary effects, and so on.

The following student example illustrates the causes and effects of ground-water contamination as discussed in an environmental science class:

Causes and Effects of Ground-Water Contamination

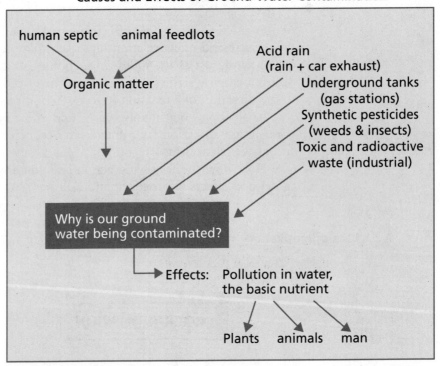

Exercise 9-B

Directions: Create an action-reaction arrow visual organizer for one of the following. Make sure your arrows point from cause to effect.

1. Why you came to college (causes).

2. What has happened to you since you've been in college — think in terms of socially, personally (i.e., self-awareness), or educationally (effects).

3. What you think the results of getting a degree will be (effects).

Ts

Ts are the appropriate visual organizer to use if you have only two items to compare or contrast, if you are preparing to write an argumentative or persuasive paper, or if you are trying to make a decision between two choices. This diagram gets the name T because of its visual shape. To create this visual organizer, you draw a line down the middle of the paper, draw an intersecting line across it at the top, and enter one item on one side of the center line and the other on the opposite side. Thus, the diagram looks like a T, and it is equated with the middle finger in our mnemonic device in a *kindly* way, because the middle finger is the midpoint of the fingers and thumb.

You can also think of the T as a balanced equation: Whatever information you put on one side of the T can usually be balanced with comparable information on the other side. Notice in the following example how the bits of information on one side are balanced by opposite information on the other side:

Pros and Cons of Returning to College

Pro	Con
Continuing my education	College may have little impact on getting a job
Eventually may end up w/ better-paying job	Will have to cut expenses now
Age provides motivation and life experience	Fear of competing w/ younger students
Can get student loan	Expensive
Reach my long-term goal	Time-consuming
Meet new people	Takes time out of my social life
Mental challenges	Added stress

In making a decision or thinking through a persuasive argument, no matter which side you favor, pro or con, you should understand the information on both sides.

You can also use a T as a prewriting technique for a comparison/contrast essay. In addition, it can act as a study guide to summarize conflicting theories or opinions.

Here is an example of a T created from a student's lecture notes in a world history course. Notice how the student begins with a two-sided question.

Has Marxism hindered or helped Africa's development?	
Viewpoint 1 **Marxism Has Hindered Africa**	**Viewpoint 2** **Marxism Has Helped Africa**
Ndabaningi Sithole	Brenda Powers
Marxist govts. (colonialism) betray Africa's people	Capitalists need colonies to keep economies afloat
Africans are opposed to Marxism—foreign European ideology	Capitalists still use imperialism to make themselves wealthier while making Africa poorer
Africans want to choose social order based on African traditions—pure, simple	Socialism would put needs of people first, offering the only real hope for Afr.
Imperialism = imposition	Social. creates conditions in which nation. div./race discr. are abolished
Marx. soc. destroyed one Afr. econ. after another—mils. die/starve	Marx. teaches that soc. revol. leads to complete elimination of natl. oppression

Webs

Webs can take many shapes, and in the hand mnemonic, the fourth finger, the ring finger, represents this type of visual organizer. Typically, a web begins with a central idea on the paper, which can be likened to a ring on the ring finger. This type of diagram lends itself well to creative thinking

Exercise 9-C

Directions: Draw a T using the following information about football and soccer.

Among sports in the United States, football is one of the most popular, but soccer has been gaining in popularity. These sports can be compared and contrasted in several ways.

The first set of rules for soccer, which is called football in most countries except the United States, was established in 1863. Currently, a team consists of 11 players, only one of whom, the goaltender, can use his or her hands. Everyone else on the team can use any other part of his or her body—feet, knees, elbows, hips, and head—to get the ball to the goal. The ball, made of leather or rubber, weighs 14 to 16 ounces and is 27 to 28 inches in circumference. The fields can be 100 to 130 yards long and 50 to 100 yards wide, but the length always has to be greater than the width. Game time varies, but professional games last 90 minutes, broken into two halves. The governing body is the *Federation Internationale de Football Association* (FIFA), and international playoffs between the top teams of each country compete in the World Cup.

Football evolved slowly from the sport rugby in the nineteenth century. The first intercollegiate game was played in 1867 between Rutgers and Princeton. The ball is an oblate spheroid, 11 to 11¼ inches long and 21¼ to 21½ inches around its longest axis. It weighs 14 to 15 ounces and is often called a "pigskin" because that is what it was originally made of, although footballs are now made of leather or plastic, with leather laces on one side, making it easy to grip the ball for carrying or passing. There are 11 players. The ball is kicked to start the game or to make field goals or extra points; otherwise, it is thrown from one player to another or carried to the goal line. The field is 100 yards long (with two additional 10-yard areas called end zones) and is 53⅓ yards wide. Professional games are 60 minutes, divided into 4 quarters, but the actual game time is much longer because the clock is stopped for various reasons. The first professional organization, the National Football League (NFL), was established in 1919. In 1946 the American Football League (AFL) was formed, and the Super Bowl, first played in 1969, is the yearly highlight of professional football.

In addition, many differences exist in the rules, scoring, and manner of play of soccer and football.

and is often best used when brainstorming for an essay or a project. Webs are easy to make and are very flexible. However, because of their open-ended structure, you may be tempted to overuse them. When a more specific visual organizer is appropriate for learning or summarizing the information, you would do well to make the more specific visual organizer.

When you create a web, you begin with a topic, a question, or a key word and branch out from there. This weblike diagram can take the shape of a tree, turkey tracks, or wheel spokes—you name it. Therefore, the resulting diagram is not as predictable in its form as some other visual organizers. It does, however, allow you to generate a great number of ideas. In the following example, using information from a psychology textbook chapter, a student created a web of the five senses in terms of stimuli (S) and receptors (R).

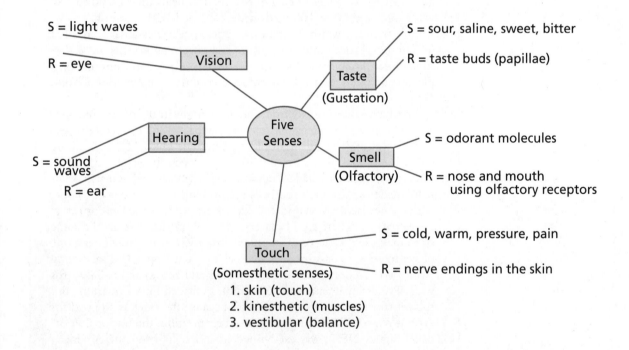

Some webs begin with a general category and move to more specific subdivisions. This pattern resembles a traditional flowchart, which is informally referred to as turkey tracks. This is a good way to narrow down a subject or to show relationships. Following is an example of such a web, using birds as the general category:

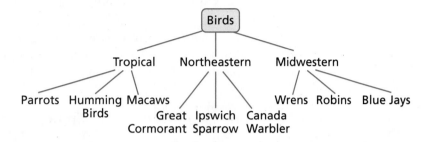

A web can take any shape that is meaningful and useful for your purposes. In such a drawing, you may use lines, as in the examples in this text, or you might make blocks, circles, or a combination of lines and geometric shapes. Whatever is meaningful to you is acceptable.

Exercise 9-D

Directions: Make a web in the shape of your choice using *one* of the following words as the main topic. Then, by brainstorming, branch out with other related words or phrases.

1. Transportation

2. Clothing

3. Historical events

4. Education

Time Lines

Time lines may be the easiest visual organizer to make, but like the little finger in the hand mnemonic, they probably will not be used as often as the other visual organizers. Time lines are limited in their use and flexibility because the information they illustrate involves time elapsed, whether it is seconds, minutes, days, years, centuries, or eras.

The structure of time lines is straightforward and fairly simple. They represent chronological events along a straight line, which can be drawn horizontally or vertically. Time lines are good visual organizers if you need to know when various events or steps in a process occur. For example, they could be used in a biology course when you are studying a process that changes fairly rapidly over a period of minutes, hours, or days. Following is an illustration of the development of an embryo during the first week after conception:

Time Line of Week 1 of Embryo Development

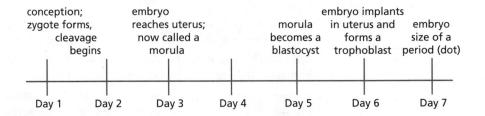

Exercise 9-E

Directions: Make a time line for the following information.

The length of gestation for various mammals and marsupials varies greatly. Old World monkeys give birth in six months (between 170 and 190 days). Gorillas, orangutans, and humans give birth in nine months. It takes the woolly monkey 225 days, but the marmoset reproduces in 140 days. Marsupials give birth in 12 to 37 days, but the baby stays in a pouch for much longer. Mouse lemurs, small members of the monkey family, give birth in two months.

Using time lines is vital in history courses, where much of the content involves dates and events. For instance, if you were studying the British monarchy from 1820 to the turn of the century, your time line might look like this:

A Time Line of Monarchs of Great Britain

1820-----------George IV

1830--------William IV

* 1832---------Reform Bill
   (right to vote)

1837------------Victoria

* Called the Victorian Age

1901-------------Edward VII

This time line is drawn vertically, but it could just as easily have been drawn horizontally. The lengths of the line between each pair of monarchs visually suggests the length of each one's rule.

The time line could also include key words that provide other important information about what happened during that period (note examples.)

This time line could be extended as you study events that occurred in the 1900s.

In conclusion, time lines can be used as a visual organizer whenever you need to know chronological information or steps in a process.

Supplementary visual organizer exercises
Exercise 9-F

Directions: Read the following selections and then create the most appropriate visual organizers.

1. The two major economies in the world are the market or capitalist economy and the centrally planned or command economy. Although variations exist in the role government and individuals play in both economies, the broadest differences involve ownership of physical capital and resource allocation. In a market economy, indi-

(continued on the next page)

Exercise 9-F (continued)

viduals have property rights. In other words, they have the ability to buy and sell goods, and this right provides incentives. In a command economy, the government owns everything, and so individuals do not have a personal incentive to invent new products, for example. In addition, in a market economy, most prices for goods are "freely determined by individuals and firms." In a command economy, the government establishes most of the prices. Many individuals or companies compete in buying and selling in a market economy. The command economy is run by a central government that often allows only one producer of an item or product, which eliminates competition. Another difference is that market economies freely trade in other countries, which can improve their own economy. Command economies are limited in their ability to buy foreign goods. The greater freedom allowed in a market economy makes it (capitalism) more appealing to many countries than a command economy (centrally planned by the government).

(Taylor 57–63)

2. In the late 1950s, two physicians began what is now called the New York Longitudinal Study, interviewing parents and observing children from birth to adolescence. They defined "easy" and "difficult" one-year-old children and "easy" and "difficult" ten-year-old children by their individual differences and temperaments.

   For example, easy one-year-olds have a regular rhythm to their lives: They nap after lunch each day and always take a bottle when they go to bed at night. Difficult one-year-olds tend to lie awake after they are put to bed; sometimes they will not fall asleep for more than an hour. Easy ten-year-olds tend to eat only at mealtimes and regularly sleep the same amount of time every night. Difficult ten-year-olds have an irregular rhythm to their lives. Their food intake varies; they may be snackers or refuse to eat at mealtime. They also vary when they will go to bed, falling asleep at different times on different nights. Easy one-year-olds have a positive attitude about new situations. They are not afraid of strangers and will readily approach them. If they have to sleep in different surroundings (at grandma's or at a friend's house), they fall asleep and sleep well. Difficult one-year-olds cry or refuse to fall asleep in a new place. Easy ten-year-olds love to go to camp, and the first time they go skiing or do other new activities they enjoy doing them. Difficult ten-year-

(continued on the next page)

Exercise 9-F (continued)

olds get very homesick if they go to camp, and they are unwilling to try new activities. In terms of adaptability, easy one-year-olds might be frightened of toy animals at first, but learn to enjoy playing with them fairly quickly. Difficult one-year-olds refuse to try new foods every time they are offered. Ten-year-olds who are adaptable might be homesick when they first get to camp but quickly learn to enjoy it. They are enthusiastic about learning everything. Nonadaptive ten-year-olds do not adjust well to new situations, whether it is camp, a new school, or even a new teacher. (Dworetzky 115)

3. All people, at least once in a while, feel fatigued because they have stayed up to watch the late, late show. However, it is helpful to look at four other reasons why fatigue occurs. One reason is emotional and stress-related: You are overworked or upset over a problem, and you worry about the problem instead of getting a good night's sleep. Your physical state may also be a source of fatigue. Maybe you do not get enough physical exercise, or maybe you are suffering from an illness such as diabetes, kidney or liver disease, or anemia. You need to see your doctor if you suspect you have such an illness. Another source of fatigue might be your diet. If you do not eat well enough, consider taking a multivitamin. Even if you do eat a balanced meal, your body is robbed of some nutrients when you undergo serious, long-lasting bouts of stress. Sleep habits are another source of fatigue. You need to set up a rhythm: Go to bed and arise at approximately the same times each day, avoid caffeine or alcohol in the evening, and know how many hours of sleep you need so that you do not get too many or too few hours per night. It is also helpful not to work on difficult mental tasks right before bedtime.

Summary

This chapter has provided you with a variety of visual organizers that you can use for different kinds of information. Using the fingers of the hand as a mnemonic device, five different visual organizers are explained and pictorially represented.

The five visual organizers are the topic grid (the thumb), action-reaction arrows (the index finger), Ts (the middle finger), webs (the ring finger), and times lines (the little finger). Grids are appropriate when you are trying to organize information that is naturally broken into two or more categories. Action-reaction arrows work well to illustrate cause-and-effect relationships. Ts serve as an excellent device to analyze two opposing views or contrasting ideas. Webs, because they are very open-ended and creative, are most useful as a prewriting activity and as a way to see relationships among concepts. Time lines help you see when events in time occurred and how they relate to one another.

Chapter 10

The Power of Taking Tests

"Testing, testing, testing. One, two, three, testing." When you hear these words, you often anticipate that something exciting and positive is about to happen. On the other hand, when you hear a teacher use a four-letter word like *test, quiz,* or *exam,* you often dread what is to come.

Testing is an integral part of education, since it provides both you and the instructor with a good indication of how much you have learned. Thus, it is to your advantage to develop the necessary skills to become an effective test taker. This chapter will review methods that should enable you to be more successful on tests. It will also discuss how to prepare for tests, how to take tests, how to minimize test anxiety, and how to analyze test results.

TYPES OF TESTS

Tests can be divided into three categories: objective, short-answer, and essay. *Objective tests* are recognition tests, which means that the possible answers are provided for you. They include true-false, multiple-choice, and matching tests. The second type of test, *short-answer,* requires you to supply a brief answer, from a phrase to a few sentences. These include completions and definitions. Finally, the *essay test* requires single-paragraph or multi-paragraph answers.

Different types of tests require you as a college student to demonstrate different skills and different levels of comprehension. You need to

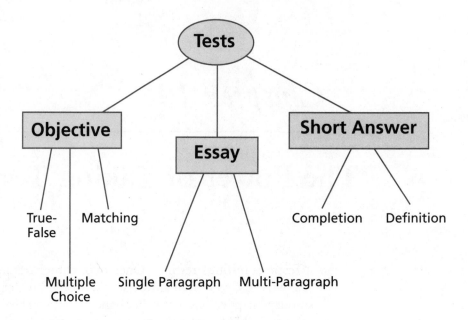

be aware that literal, factual questions are only one type of question that instructors ask. They may also ask more complicated questions, such as application questions. Application questions require you to reexamine information that you have studied in a class and put it to use in a different situation. On a test in a nursing course, you might be given a list of a patient's symptoms. Your task on this test would be to consider the patient's history and the list of symptoms in order to identify the patient's problem and to write a nursing care plan. In an English class, after reading Maya Angelou's autobiography *I Know Why the Caged Bird Sings*, you might be asked to write an essay that discusses how the events of the author's early life influenced her writing.

ON YOUR MARK: WHAT YOU ALREADY KNOW

Each quarter, starting on the first day of class, you will naturally begin by taking GREAT notes (see Chapter 1), using STUDY-READ (see Chapter 3), and learning new terms (see Chapter 4). By keeping up with your reading assignments and reviewing your notes, you will be preparing for quizzes and laying the groundwork for taking bigger tests. By reciting

answers to your questions until you have learned the material, you will have stored that information in your long-term memory, where it will be readily retrievable during exams. Memory techniques (see Chapter 8) and your personal visual organizers (see Chapter 9) provide you with additional ways to store information for easy retrieval.

As midterm or final exams approach, your priority—weekly, daily, and hourly—is to get the most out of your time in order to stay on target and avoid undue stress. Just as a runner in training has a daily regimen, the study skills you have employed thus far are your daily regimen for learning. As a test, midterm, or final approaches, you, again like the runner, will move into a more intensified program of study and time management. Beginning one to two weeks before a major exam, it is a good idea to include extra, concentrated study time for preparation in your regular study schedule (see Chapter 7). By adhering to this schedule, you can avoid cramming and test anxiety. These study sessions should focus on recitation and review. This is best accomplished by reciting answers to your questions in your texts and notes, by making and studying your own visual organizers, and by reviewing your vocabulary terms.

GET SET: ACQUIRING A WINNER'S EDGE

When you are facing a major test or exam, you, like the experienced athlete, want to gain all the honest advantages you can. You want to be test-smart, to be well versed enough to know what to expect.

As the exam draws closer, ask your instructor what the test format will be—true-false, multiple-choice, matching, essay, short-answer, etc.

Often tests, especially midterms and finals, have several formats. The more you know about the construction of the test, the more comfortable you will be as you prepare for and take the test. Furthermore, once you know the format, you can make up practice questions and prepare visual organizers.

As you make visual organizers and recite information, work in your regular study place, free from noise and distractions. Reciting answers aloud will confirm to you that you really do know the information and will further strengthen your knowledge base.

You may also find that studying with a partner or a small group is helpful because it gives each of you an opportunity to share notes, information, and ideas. Also, you can weigh and compare what each of you determines is important. Together you can make up study questions and share techniques to help you remember concepts and bodies of information. If you do work in a group, make sure that each member is willing to contribute and that you have an organizational plan to keep you on track.

Sufficient preparation means that you will not have to cram at the last minute. Cramming is usually an exercise in futility. It's like overloading an electrical system. If you try to put too much information into your

brain at once, it will overload the short-term circuitry, and you may experience the equivalent of a loss of power or a blackout. In other words, you may not be able to recall the information when you most need it.

One final step in preparing for exams is to have a positive attitude. Some students actually flunk themselves by thinking they are going to fail. One method of preparation you can use is to visualize your success. Imagine yourself taking the test and doing well. As you visualize, focus on the many, many right answers you are able to write down. Just as quarterbacks visualize the perfect pass, basketball players visualize perfect dunk shots, golfers visualize good putts, and pitchers visualize the perfect curve ball, so should you visualize your victory before you even begin the test.

GO: TAKING THE TEST

Athletes, even knowing that they are in good condition and well prepared, will naturally feel tension at the starting signal. Likewise, when you are faced with actually taking a test, you may well experience exam

nerves. Being somewhat nervous can be positive stress, which is good because it pumps up your adrenaline and makes you more alert.

On the test day, be sure to arrive on time or a little early so that you will not feel rushed. Have an extra pen or pencil and any other equipment you might need, such as extra blue books. While you are waiting for the exam to begin, use the stress-reducing exercise from Chapter 6, or just take several deep breaths. This will help calm any jitters you might have and get more oxygen—thinking power—to your brain.

When your instructor distributes the exam, jot down "slippery" facts in the margin or on the back of the test. *Slippery facts* are those words, formulas, dates, or other information you are *sure* you will forget. (Of course, check with your instructor in advance to find out if you are allowed to write on the test itself.) Writing down this information will keep you from worrying about forgetting it because it will be there if you need it.

Despite your eagerness to begin the test, listen carefully to any last-minute instructions the teacher gives. Next, look over the whole test to get an overview of its parts and length and how many points each section is worth; then plan your time accordingly. As you take the test, follow your time schedule as best you can rather than getting bogged down trying to remember an answer.

As you approach each section, read the written instructions very carefully. You may even want to read them twice. If you are allowed to write on the test, circle or underline important words. Too often students waste valuable time or lose points on a test because they do not follow directions. For example, if the directions read, "Answer only three of the five essay questions," and you answer all five questions, you will be wasting your time. Or if the directions say, "Write out the words 'true' and 'false' when answering the following questions," and you simply write the letters T and F, you may lose points. The few minutes it takes to read the directions may result in a higher score.

You do not have to start at the beginning of the test. If one particular part of the test seems easier than another part, start with the easier part and answer the questions that you are sure you know. Mark any questions you have omitted so that you can go back and answer them later. Giving correct answers early in the test will build your confidence and help you keep a positive attitude. In addition, as you go through the whole test and complete answers you know, "forgotten" answers may pop into your mind. Also, some other questions on the exam may provide clues to the answers you were unable to think of earlier. When you have answered all the questions you know, go back to the ones you omitted. When all else fails, you should use logic and educated guesswork to answer any remaining questions. These techniques will be explained later in this chapter.

If you are using a scantron form to record your answers, skipping around may not be a good idea because that could lead you to mark an answer in the wrong place. Whether or not you omit answers on a scantron, be very careful to record your answers in the correct place.

If you finish an exam early, do not turn in your test and leave until you have checked your answers carefully. Other students may leave early, but you should not be influenced by them. After all, they may be leaving because they have given up. If you have extra time, use it wisely. First, go back over your exam, rereading the directions and checking your answers. Do not change your answers, though, unless you have a valid reason for doing so. When you are unsure of an answer, your first response is usually right. In addition, you should allow time to clarify, add information, correct spelling, or fix other errors.

TAKING OBJECTIVE TESTS

Objective tests, where the possible answers appear on the test paper, include true-false, multiple-choice, and matching tests. For obvious reasons, most students are more comfortable with these test questions than with other types. However, in order to be test-smart, you can still benefit from some helpful tips on taking these types of tests.

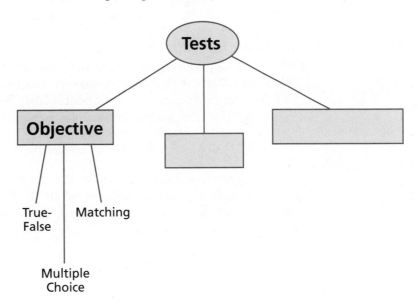

True-False Tests

True-false tests can be the least threatening type of test to take because you have a fifty-fifty chance of answering the questions correctly—excellent odds, even in Las Vegas. Even when you know the material thoroughly, you can increase your chances of answering the questions correctly by being aware of certain reading and test-taking techniques. These techniques include:

- All-or-nothing words and in-between words
- Negative words
- Partial truths
- Fifty-fifty chance

All-or-Nothing Words and In-Between Words   At first glance, true-false tests may seem easy; however, students often complain that some teachers purposely write "tricky" true-false items. So-called tricky items may simply include qualifying words that have a dramatic impact on the trueness or falseness of the statement. If you are aware of these words and read the items carefully, you should have no problem answering true-false items correctly, assuming that you know the information. These dramatic qualifying words can be divided into two types: all-or-nothing words and in-between words. Examples of all-or-nothing words include words like:

all	always	none	never	nothing	every
		exactly	invariably		

What these words have in common is that they are so powerful that they allow no exceptions. Therefore, when you come across these words, or others like them, it should be a wake-up call because the lack of exceptions will generally mean the statement is false. For example, examine the following statement and determine if it is true or false:

T   F   All cars and trucks must have license plates.

At first glance this statement may seem true, but exceptions do exist.

Although *most* all-or-nothing words do indicate false statements, you still must apply logic as you read. For example, think about this statement:

T   F   All presidents and vice presidents of the U.S. have been men.

In this case, the answer is true, as you all know. Although most all-or-nothing statements will be false, a few may be true.

When other qualifying words, called in-between words, are placed in a sentence, they modify or alter the meaning of the true-false statement to indicate possible exceptions. Some examples of in-between words include:

few	frequently	generally	many	most	often
	sometimes	seldom	usually	probably	

When taking a true-false test, be aware of in-between words because statements containing in-between words are almost always true. Look at the following example:

T   F   Usually cars and trucks must have license plates.

If you are aware of the all-or-nothing and in-between words as you take a test, you can significantly increase your ability to read and answer these questions. If you are allowed to write on the test, it is a good idea to circle or underline qualifying words as an additional aid to remembering their significance.

Negative Words   Another important reading technique to help you correctly answer true-false items involves an awareness of negative words. If you read a true-false item too quickly, you may overlook negative words and come to a wrong conclusion. As with qualifying words, if you are allowed to write on the test, circle or underline the negative words to make them stand out.

Negative words include simple ones, such as:

cannot   does not   is not   will not

Other negatives are found in prefixes, such as:

il- (illogical)   *un-* (unreasonable)   *ir-* (irregular)
im- (impossible)   *non-* (nonstandard)   *in-* (incorrect)

Be especially careful if two negative words appear in a true-false statement. They will cancel each other out and make the double negative statement positive. Using your awareness of negative words, read the following three statements and determine whether they are true or false:

T   F   1. In a typical year, 25 to 50 million Americans catch the flu.

T   F   2. During a nontypical year, 25 to 50 million Americans catch the flu.

T   F   3. It is not uncommon for 25 to 50 million Americans per year to catch the flu.

According to an article in the *Cincinnati Enquirer*'s *USA Weekend* (January 5–7, 1996), 25 to 50 million Americans catch the flu each year; therefore, the first statement is true. Since the first statement is true, the second statement is false because of the prefix *non-*. The third statement is also true. This sentence has two negatives (*not* and the prefix *un-*) that cancel each other out and make the statement true.

Partial Truths   If any part of a true-false statement is incorrect, then the whole statement is false. Test-taking traps involving such partial truths generally occur in two situations: (1) items in a series and (2) a faulty relationship of words in a sentence. Read the following examples:

T   F   1. The Atlantic coastal states, sometimes subject to devastating hurricanes, are Florida, Georgia, North Carolina, South Carolina, and Washington.

T   F   2. When John F. Kennedy was forty, he won the Pulitzer Prize for his book *Profiles in Courage;* consequently, at age forty-three he became the youngest President of the United States.

In the first example, a series of items (the states), is listed; however, the state of Washington is not on the Atlantic Coast; it is on the Pacific. Thus, the whole statement is false. In the second example, both facts are accurate, but the connector, the word *consequently,* makes the whole statement false. The first fact did not cause the second one to happen.

Fifty-fifty Chance   One last strategy to keep in mind when taking a true-false test is that you have a fifty-fifty chance of being correct when you answer a question. Therefore, be sure that you answer all the questions rather than leaving any blanks.

Multiple-Choice Tests

Multiple-choice items are made up of two elements: the *stem*, which is an incomplete statement or a question, and the *options*, which are the choices that complete the statement or answer the question.

In order to do well on a multiple-choice test, first, it is important to read the stem slowly and carefully. The stem contains the basic information that helps you understand what is being asked. Thus, you need to look for key words, all-or-nothing or in-between words, and negative words. You may want to underline or circle them if you are allowed to write on the test. This active method of reading helps you to focus your attention and to read accurately and precisely.

Second, as you read the options, be sure to read *all* of them with an open mind before you begin eliminating possible choices. Consider all the possibilities and do not cross out one or more of them too hastily.

Sometimes you may know the correct answer immediately, but if you are not sure, you may find the following approach useful. To begin, read the stem with each option as if the stem and option together make a true or false statement. As you read each option, mark it T or F or ?, assuming you can write on the test. (If you cannot mark on the test, do this mentally.) This process of reading and eliminating should produce the correct answer, or at least increase your odds of being correct.

Two options typically used in multiple-choice tests are "all of the above" and "none of the above." Using the T or F or ? method described above, you should be able to determine if more than one option is correct. If you have found more than one correct answer among the other choices, then "all of the above" is probably the correct choice. On the other hand, "none of the above" is seldom the correct choice. Most teachers would not want to make up a question with all wrong answers. They may simply be including "none of the above" to create the required number of options.

On some tests, the choices may include combined options, such as "both A and B are correct" or "both B and D are correct." In such cases, you will again benefit by using the stem and option T or F or ? method to make your choices.

Matching Tests

In format, a matching test usually consists of two columns of items: the base column, often designated by numbers, and the choices column, often designated by letters.

When taking a matching test, follow these guidelines:

- Scan both columns to determine if the two contain the same number of items. That way you will know whether extra choices exist.
- If extra choices do exist, you would do well to begin with the base-column items and find their matches in the choices column.
- If the number of choices is equal, then you may begin with either column.
- Always match the items you absolutely know first, marking off each choice as you select it. This narrows the remaining possibilities and will save you time.
- Rather than leaving any answers blank, use your logic and knowledge of the course to complete any answers you temporarily skipped.
- Sometimes the wording or grammatical clues will give you a hint as to what type of match from the choices column is expected. For example, the base-column items might indicate that the match is the name of a person, a date, a definition, a function, a theory, and so on.

TAKING SHORT-ANSWER TESTS

Short-answer tests can be a bit more challenging and unsettling than objective tests because the answers do not appear on the exam. It is up to you to provide the answers—a word, a phrase, or one or more sentences. Short-answer questions include completions and definitions.

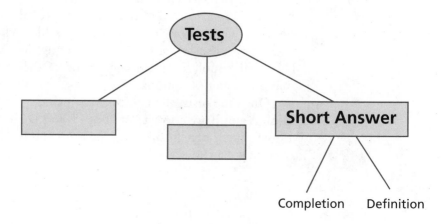

Completions

Completion or fill-in-the-blank tests require you to know the information extremely well and to be able to recognize the clues in each statement. The statement itself will give you clues to what kind of answer is expected—a name, a place, an action, a date, a term, a list, etc. Sometimes other clues—the length of the blank or the number of spaces—will indicate the length of the answer or the number of words required. For example, if the question on a biology test is, "The main water-conducting cells of xylem are called _____ and _____," you know you are required to fill in names of cells, in this case the words *trachieds* and *vessel members*. As another example, if the question reads, "The scientific method used when gathering information includes _____, _____, and _____," you should be able to determine that three kinds of actions are needed, in this case *hypothesizing, predicting,* and *testing*.

If you are unable to complete a fill-in-the-blank item, you may find clues to the answer in some other part of the test.

Definitions

In the category of short-answer tests, another type is definitions of terms. A fail-safe way to be able to write definitions is to learn the terms thoroughly by reviewing them frequently throughout the quarter.

When you are defining words on a test, the best method is to write complete sentences, unless you are instructed otherwise. In order to do this, combine the term with a verb and give the meaning of the term as clearly as possible. Write the sentence(s) without using the term itself in the definition. Think of this formula:

Term + Verb + Meaning without Using Term

For instance, instead of writing, "Recitation means to recite," write, "Recitation means saying the information aloud, in your own words, often enough to store it in your long-term memory." Instead of writing, "Sensory learning refers to using your senses," you could write, "Sensory learning refers to the use of sound, sight, and/or touch to improve your memory, such as by writing your notes (touch), reading your notes (sight), and reciting them aloud (sound)." Notice that in this last definition, the meaning is clarified by the use of an example. Including an example in your definition strengthens your answer by proving that you truly understand the term.

TAKING ESSAY TESTS

Sometimes students panic at the thought of taking essay tests. However, an essay exam need not be intimidating as long as you know the information thoroughly and know how to organize the material.

When you hear the words "essay test," you need to know what your instructor means. Some instructors may expect answers of a single paragraph; others may be expecting multi-paragraph essays. Some may expect a factual answer; others may expect an application answer.

Regardless of what kind of essay question is asked or how long the answer is expected to be, you must be able to budget your time in order to answer all the questions thoroughly. If you have more than one essay question to answer, start with the one that seems easiest to you because you will gain self-confidence, you will be able to respond quickly, and you will be ready to focus on more challenging questions.

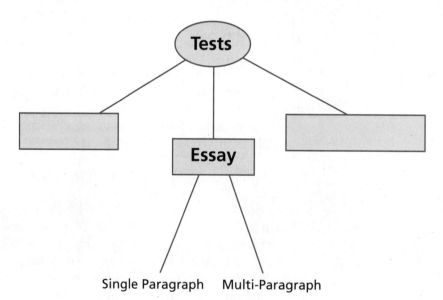

Directional Words

Writing an essay of any length requires that you read the question carefully, looking for directional words. *Directional words* are verbs that indicate what kind of information should be included and how it should be delivered. In other words, the directional words tell you what information the teacher expects you to provide and the format you should use. For example, each of the following directional words requires you to write your answer differently:

analyze: Break the topic into its logical parts and write about each one.

compare: Show likenesses (although some instructors use the word to mean compare and contrast—check to make sure).

contrast: Show differences.

criticize, discuss, and *evaluate:* Give both positive and negative aspects of the subject and then draw your conclusion(s).

describe and *explain:* Make the topic clear by giving the major details and supporting facts.

illustrate: Explain by giving examples.

interpret: Clarify the meaning or paraphrase the information.

justify: Explain the purpose behind or reasons for a statement.

prove: Provide evidence in the form of facts and details to confirm an assertion.

relate: Reveal connections between or among subjects.

summarize: Give the main points.

trace: Show the development or history of the subject chronologically.

Reducing an Essay to Mini-Questions

Besides focusing on the directional words as you read the essay question, it is important to notice whether the question has more than one part, that is, has *mini-questions*. For example, in an American history course a question might read:

> "Explain the significance of the Civil War one year after it ended in terms of the economy and the social repercussions in both the North and the South and give examples of each."

Stop for a minute and reread that question. How many questions are contained in this large question? If you underline the directional words and key words and number the mini-questions, your essay question will look like this:

"Explain the significance of the Civil War one year after it ended in terms of the economy in the North (1st question) and South (2nd question) and the social repercussions in the North (3rd question) and South (4th question) and give examples of each" (questions 5 through 8 because you need four examples).

As you can see, this question actually has eight parts, all of which need to be addressed in your answer. By numbering each mini-question, you can make sure you answer all of them.

As soon as you have determined the mini parts of the question, jot them down in the margin of your test or blue book. You may want to use a web or some other informal diagram. For example, for the question above, your web might look something like this:

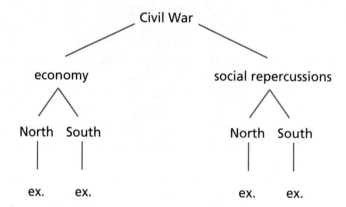

This web will guide you in writing your essay. By clustering ideas, you can determine how many paragraphs you will need and the logical organization of your ideas.

Exercise 10-A

Directions: Read the following essay question and underline the directional words and key words. Number the mini-questions.

Using the acronym for the reasons for procrastination in Chapter 7, explain the four basic reasons why people procrastinate. For each reason, give a solution (without duplicating them).

Now, on a piece of paper, draw a web or other informal diagram as a guide for writing the essay (you do not have to write the essay).

Writing the Essay Answer

Once you have an organizational plan, you are ready to write your opening statement or opening paragraph. That statement is called a *topic sentence* for a one-paragraph answer or a *thesis statement* within an introductory paragraph for a multiparagraph essay. In essence, what you will do is turn the essay question into a general statement. In the Civil War example, your statement might be:

> "In 1866, the Civil War had a great impact on the economy and created social repercussions in both the North and the South."

Then, following the organization you established in your thesis statement (or topic sentence) and informal outline, begin writing the body paragraphs of your essay. Write your answer as if you were explaining the subject to a person who knows nothing about it so that you will be as clear, complete, and precise as possible in your answer. Include as many facts, definitions, examples, details, and other information as needed. Write a concluding sentence or paragraph at the end of the essay to wrap up your answer.

When you have more than one essay question to answer, be sure to budget your time accordingly. If, for example, you have three questions to answer and you spend all your time answering only one, even if your answer is very complete, that answer is only one-third of the test. If you do not answer the other two questions, you will fail the test.

If you have miscalculated and you run out of time before you have completed all of your essay answers, rather than leaving a question unanswered or only partly finished, outline the answer as best you can. That way your instructor will understand that you know the major points even though you were not able to write or complete the essay. By outlining, you might get partial credit for an answer.

Finally, if you finish early, do not turn in your test immediately. Use that extra time wisely to proofread your answers, cleaning up any spelling errors, checking your punctuation, and neatly inserting omitted words or added information.

Additional Tips for Grade Enhancement

- Write on every other line in case you have time to go back and add more information.

- Leave space between answers in case you think of something that you want to add.
- Write only on the right-hand page of the blue book and number your pages.
- Write legibly.
- Use an erasable ball-point pen rather than a pencil.
- Indent your paragraphs and leave one-inch margins on both sides of the paper.

TEST ANXIETY

Many students suffer from test anxiety. Basically, anxiety is extreme fear of a danger or fear of the unknown. *Test anxiety* is fear of not measuring up to expectations—either your own or another person's.

The very best confidence builder and cure for test anxiety is to be thoroughly prepared for the test. This means regular recitation and review over a period of time, not cramming the night before.

Even if you are thoroughly prepared, don't be surprised if you feel a little nervous. That's only natural. Focus on the test itself, not on your feelings of stress. Remember that positive stress can give you a surge of adrenaline, which will clarify your thoughts and actually help you perform better.

Here are some additional ways to relieve test anxiety:

- Find out as much about the test as you can—length, types of test questions, point distribution, time allowed—so that you won't be surprised when you see the actual test.
- Arrive a few minutes early so that you won't feel rushed and so that you will hear any directions the instructor gives.
- Relax—take deep breaths before you start the test.
- Use positive self-talk.
- After you receive the test, jot down slippery facts (any formulas, dates, information, or ideas you think you might forget).
- Read all the directions carefully before you begin the test.
- Make a time plan, budgeting time for each section in accordance with how many points the section is worth.
- Answer easy questions first.
- Use your test-taking strategies to make informed choices.
- Don't be distracted by students who leave early.

COPING WITH TEST RESULTS

How many times have you seen a student get back a test that he or she failed or did poorly on, moan and groan, wad up the offending test, and throw it in the nearest wastebasket? Maybe you have done that yourself. It's a natural reaction, but not a very helpful one. Instead of expressing your disappointment by throwing your test away, you should analyze your results in order to improve future test scores.

To begin your analysis of a test you have taken, look at the test items you missed. Try to find patterns. What kinds of questions did you miss? For example, did you miss true-false items, multiple-choice items, definitions, completions, essays? Then analyze the patterns of errors. What caused you to miss those questions? Did you misread the question? Did you study the wrong material? Or could other factors have caused you to score poorly on the test? For example, did you not plan and/or use your time realistically?

You can use the following chart to analyze your test results:

Test Analysis

Directions: Look at the test you have taken to determine which types of questions you most often missed. Then read the statements below, and put a check mark in front of each factor that influenced your test results.

Objective Test Items
- ☐ I ignored all-or-nothing words.
- ☐ I ignored negative prefixes or words.
- ☐ I did not consider all parts of the statement.
- ☐ I left test items blank.
- ☐ I ignored key words.
- ☐ I jumped to a conclusion before reading the entire question.
- ☐ I did not eliminate options using the T-F-? in multiple-choice.
- ☐ I did not use a logical process of elimination.

Short-Answer Questions
- ☐ I did not take advantage of clues on completion questions.
- ☐ I wrote in fragments instead of complete sentences.
- ☐ I used the term itself to define a term.
- ☐ My answer was not specific enough.

(continued on the next page)

Test Analysis (continued)

Essays
- ☐ My essay was poorly organized.
- ☐ I did not develop my ideas fully.
- ☐ I used unsubstantiated opinions or generalizations.
- ☐ I ignored directional words.
- ☐ I did not answer all the mini-questions within the essay question.
- ☐ My writing skills (grammar, punctuation, spelling, sentence structure) were weak.
- ☐ My essay was not neat and legible.

Test Preparation Factors
- ☐ I took inadequate notes.
- ☐ I should read and mark my text better.
- ☐ I did not recite my notes and text material to the point of mastery.
- ☐ I did not use appropriate memory techniques when studying.
- ☐ I did not prepare my own personal visual organizers.

Other Factors
- ☐ I crammed.
- ☐ I misread or did not follow directions.
- ☐ I made poor use of my time.
- ☐ I did not mark the test to focus my attention.
- ☐ My general reading comprehension was inadequate.
- ☐ I put undue stress on myself by negative self-talk.
- ☐ I allowed test anxiety to overwhelm me.
- ☐ I let a physical or emotional crisis distract me.
- ☐ I did not know the information.

Look at what you have checked on the test analysis. These are the skills, behaviors, or attitudes you need to improve before the next test.

Summary

Tests can be divided into three major categories: objective, short-answer, and essay. Regardless of the type of test, you need to begin preparing for it as soon as the quarter or semester starts. Find out as much as you can about the format of the test and prepare for it wisely, using your knowledge of study techniques and keeping a positive attitude. On the day of the test, by arriving on time, reading directions carefully, and using other test-smart techniques, you can help to ensure that you will do your best.

Objective tests, which can be true-false, multiple-choice, or matching, provide you with possible answers. As you take objective tests, be aware of all-or-nothing words and in-between words, negative words, and partial truths. Be sure to answer all questions.

Short-answer tests—completions and definitions—do not provide the answer choices; you have to supply them. Clues about what to write in completion (also called fill-in-the-blank) questions include how the sentence is worded and the length and number of blank spaces. Defining terms requires that you write a complete sentence (Term + Verb + Meaning without Using Term) and include an example if possible.

Essay tests call for answers of one or more paragraphs. Writing an essay of any length requires you to follow the directional words, to use some outlining technique to organize your answer, and to answer all the mini-questions embedded in the essay question.

Anxiety can negatively affect your performance on a test, but being prepared and using your nervousness as a positive adrenaline-building force can relieve that distress. Other ways to reduce test anxiety include physical relaxation techniques, careful reading, good time management, and focusing on the test rather than on yourself.

Finally, you need to analyze your test results in order to make a strategic plan for improving your future test-taking skills and, therefore, your grades.

Works Cited and Consulted

Boyes, William, and Michael Melvin. *Macroeconomics.* 2nd ed. Boston: Houghton Mifflin, 1994.

Chaffee, John. *Thinking Critically.* 3rd ed. Boston: Houghton Mifflin, 1991.

Dickinson, Emily. *The Complete Poems of Emily Dickinson.* Ed. Thomas H. Johnson. Boston: Little, Brown, 1960.

Dworetzky, John P. *Introduction to Child Development.* 4th ed. St. Paul, Minn.: West Publishing, 1990.

Faelten, Sharon, and David Diamond. *Take Control of Your Life.* Emmaus, Pa.: Rodale Press, 1988.

Levine, Joseph S., and Kenneth R. Miller. *Biology: Discovering Life.* 2nd ed. Lexington, Mass.: D. C. Heath, 1994.

Loftus, Elizabeth. *Memory: surprising new insights into how we remember and why we forget.* Reading, Mass.: Addison-Wesley, 1980.

Mader, Sylvia S. *Inquiry into Life.* 7th ed. Dubuque, Iowa: Wm. C. Brown, 1994.

Malcolm X as told to Alex Haley. *The Autobiography of Malcolm X.* New York: Balantine Books, 1964.

Myers, Isabel Briggs, and Mary H. McCaulley. *Manual: A Guide to the Development and Use of the Myers-Briggs Type Indicator.* Palo Alto, Calif.: Consulting Psychologists Press, 1988.

Patterson, Becky. *Concentration: Strategies for Attaining Focus.* Dubuque, Iowa: Kendal-Hunt, 1993.

Pauk, Walter. *How to Study in College.* 3rd ed. Boston: Houghton Mifflin, 1984.

Piper, Watty (retold by). *The Little Engine That Could.* From *The Pony Engine* by Mabel Bragg. New York: Platt and Munk, 1976.

Roget's The New Thesaurus. 3rd ed. by the Editors of *The American Heritage Dictionaries.* Boston: Houghton Mifflin, 1995.

Roget's International Thesaurus. 4th ed. Rev. by Robert L. Chapman. New York: Harper & Row, 1977.

Taylor, John B. *Economics.* Boston: Houghton Mifflin, 1995.

Usova, George M. *Efficient Study Strategies: Skills for Successful Learning.* Pacific Grove, Calif.: Brooks/Cole, 1989.

Index